WHO DOES GOD SEE WHEN HE SEES ME?

Dr. David Del Vecchio

DR. DAVID DEL VECCHIO

Who Does God See When He Sees Me?

© 2025 by Dr. David Del Vecchio

All rights reserved.

This book is protected under the copyright laws of the United States of America. This book may not be copied or reprinted for commercial gain or profit. The use of short quotations or occasional page copying for personal, or group study is permitted and encouraged. Permission will be granted upon request.

Dr. David Del Vecchio
Christ Church International
P.O. 5987
Dothan, Al 36302

Translations Quoted:

AMPC—Scripture quotations taken from the Amplified® Bible (AMPC), Copyright © 1954, 1958, 1962, 1964, 1965, 1987 by The Lockman Foundation. Used by permission. www.lockman.org
ESV—The ESV® Bible (The Holy Bible, English Standard Version®), © 2001 by Crossway, a publishing ministry of Good News Publishers. Used by permission. All rights reserved.
HCSB—Scripture quotations marked HCSB are taken from the Holman Christian Standard Bible®, Copyright © 1999, 2000, 2002, 2003, 2009 by Holman Bible Publishers. Used by permission. Holman Christian Standard Bible®, Holman CSB®, and HCSB® are federally registered trademarks of Holman Bible Publishers.
KJV—Scriptures marked KJV are taken from the KING JAMES VERSION (KJV): KING JAMES VERSION, public domain.
NIV—New International Version, Copyright © 1973, 1978, 1984, 2011 by International Bible Society, Zondervan Publishing House. Used by Permission
NKJV—Scripture is taken from the New King James Version®. Copyright © 1982 by Thomas Nelson. Used by permission. All rights reserved.

TABLE OF CONTENTS

FORWARD	4
CHAPTER ONE	6
CHAPTER TWO	40
CHAPTER THREE	57
CHAPTER FOUR	71
CHAPTER FIVE	97
CHAPTER SIX	128
CHAPTER SEVEN	154

DR. DAVID DEL VECCHIO

FORWARD

Here is another insightful and discerning book from David Del Vecchio. He asks the question, "whom does God see when he sees me?" His thoughtful exposition of the scriptures related to this important question are eye-opening.

David uses the New Testament Greek language effectively to inform his special insights. Here is a great quote that is indicative of this book:

> *To be in Christ – that makes you fit for heaven, but for Christ to be in you – that makes you fit for earth.*
>
> *To be in Christ – that changes your destination, but for Christ to be in you, that changes your destiny, One makes heaven your home – the other makes the world His workshop.*

I strongly recommend this book, filled with such biblical wisdom and insight as you see in this quote. Our thanks to David Del Vecchio for presenting this excellent book. It is a fresh and engaging study in spiritual development within the body of Christ.

Ronald E. Cottle, Sr.
Diploma in Theology from Southeastern Bible Institute
B.A. in English-Religion, Florida Southern College
M-Div. from Lutheran Theological Southern Seminary
Ph. D. in Religion and the M.S.Ed. and Ed. D. in Higher Education from the University of Southern California

CHAPTER ONE

Have you ever asked yourself the question; 'Who does God see when He sees me'? I want to take a walk together through the scriptures *and see if together we can* **determine what God is seeing**, **when He looks at me and He Looks at you**.

I want to begin today by going back to a conversation Jesus had with Simon Peter.

> **Luke 22:31-32 KJV (commentary added)**
>
> [31]And the Lord said, Simon, Simon, behold, Satan hath desired to have you, that he may sift you as wheat:
>
> [32]But I have prayed for thee, that thy faith, <u>fail not</u>: *[vanish or leave or stop]* and when thou art converted, *[turned back;* <u>epistrepho</u>*]* strengthen thy brethren.

Verse 31 actually says: **Simon Peter,** <u>satan has repeatedly asked Me to give you back to him,</u> *so that he can flip you around like the sifting of grain.* Picture that. That means satan wants to erase Peter's faith and make his life miserable.

This is written in the middle voice, because this is something satan wants for **himself**; this is _typical in the mind of satan_, because in his mind _it is all about him_. Jesus responded to Peter, and told him about satan's request, to give Peter back. Peter, I have prayed, *especially for you*, that when you turn over your life to Me again, strengthen and establish your brothers in the faith. Peter did not know that he had fallen back in his service and love for the Lord.

When we first read this, we did not see Peter had already fallen away from Jesus, but Jesus saw it. *Peter saw himself as the protector and upholder of Jesus.* Peter did not see himself in the same way that Jesus saw him; Jesus had a totally different view and very opposite that of Peter's.

We also find something else in these verses; we can see in these verses that Jesus would not have a need to pray *if He was at this time operating as a heavenly being, but He was not,* He was operating as a man and not deity. He prayed for Peter as opposed to just calling what He wanted forth, because the decision to walk back into the life of Jesus was up to Peter, not Jesus.

Recall Peter, in later verses *when Peter walked away from Jesus* and denied even knowing Him. Jesus is the One who said, **AGAIN**—meaning Peter's denial *took him out of the plan God had* *for him* and put him back into the vast group, who would never see heaven—the word in Greek is **EPISTREPHO,** which means return or turn back in the absolute sense and become changed into someone different.

Jesus by this action is refuting once saved always saved, and also, the idea that John Calvin left us, that if Peter or anyone of us was really born again, we would never turn back to who we were before Jesus—That thinking is repeatedly proven in the bible not to be true. **We just read it.** Not only that, but anyone who can think beyond the moment they are in, will confirm in their own life, that once saved always saved is absurd, *because the things that happen in each of our lives reveals that thinking is nonsense* and the only reason it is supported by some groups is to satisfy those who are still sinning as a habit, and cannot seem to stop and do not want to miss heaven. *And they have no active relationship with Holy Spirit.*

Concerning Peter

Matthew 26:31–35 (HCSB) *Jesus is speaking with His disciples about what is next.*

> ³¹Then Jesus said to them, "Tonight all of you will run away because of Me, for it is written:

I will strike the shepherd,
and the sheep of the flock will be scattered.

³²But after I have been resurrected, I will go ahead of you to Galilee."

³³Peter told Him, "Even if everyone runs away because of You, I will never run away!"

³⁴"I assure you," Jesus said to him, "tonight, before the rooster crows, you will deny Me three times!"

³⁵"Even if I have to die with You," Peter told Him, "I will never deny You!"

And all the disciples said the same thing. Jesus has a very different picture of Peter; much different than Peter has of himself. Peter sees himself as the victor over whatever comes next in his life and he sees himself as the answer to the problems other people have. Jesus sees Peter in a very revealed way and Jesus is working to save Peter from himself, the devil and the world, yet Peter is not aware of that until Jesus tells him.

It is Peter who is leading the charge in this exchange of words, but be assured that all the disciples felt the same way, and we read that in verse 35, yet they all did indeed leave Jesus, because of more than fear, because of doubt. They doubted in their hearts that Jesus was the Son of God, as they had all previously agreed He was, and I say that, because when He did not do what they expected from Him, they doubted who He was.

So, indeed here we see men who were sold out to Christ, had a change of heart and walked away from Christ, even if it was only for several days. If in their hearts they really believed He was the Son of God, they would have known just like the rest of us, that we are to stand pat, and see what He as the Son will do next, but we very often do not believe or trust even what we say we do, and we run away or complain or question Him or His actions, as if we knew something He does not know.

Read about this again, about this failure to hold onto what we say we believe when Paul speaks to the church he started in Galatia, *concerning those who **walked back** their decision to follow Christ.*

Galatians 3:1–4 NKJV (commentary added)

> [1]O foolish Galatians! Who has bewitched you that you should not obey the truth, before whose eyes Jesus Christ was clearly portrayed

among you as crucified? ²This only I want to learn from you: Did you receive the Spirit by the works of the law, or by the hearing of faith? *[they received the Spirit by faith; in other words, they were born-again]*³Are you so foolish? Having begun in the Spirit, are you now being made perfect by the flesh? ⁴Have you suffered so many things in vain—if indeed it was in vain?

Vain means absolutely without purpose, unprofitable, good for nothing.

What did Jesus say about the unprofitable servant?

Read it with me in Matthew's work.

Matthew 25:30 HCSB

> ³⁰And throw this good-for-nothing slave into the outer darkness. In that place there will be weeping and gnashing of teeth.

He was not an outsider; he was a servant or slave from the house of the master. He was a *doulos'*, a slave or servant in permanent service to a master. Peter is also a *doulos'*, or we have considered him to be one, and so were the other 11 apostles, daily found in the service of Jesus, because after nearly three years when others speak about Jesus, they would also mention his servants, referring to the other men who were in service with Jesus.

Jesus has been with his disciples over 30 months; they have under his direct tutelage, healed the sick, cast out demons, prophesied and performed other miracles. I believe it is safe to say they had committed to Christ and made numerous professions of acceptance of Jesus as Lord. Each and every day they faced the challenges of being the first men on earth, other than Jesus, who are healing the sick, casting out demons and telling the world the good news about Jesus and that this new life can be theirs as well. Yet at the end of his discussion, with these who had committed and called Jesus Lord, and made public profession of their faith, Jesus said to Peter.

Luke 22:32

> [32]But I have prayed for thee, that thy faith fail not: and when thou art *converted*, strengthen thy brethren.

> *1994 epistrepho (ep-ee-stref'-o); turn your way back to God to reverse the path, you are taking (literally, figuratively or morally):* <u>it would appear that somewhere along the way, Peter became an unprofitable servant.</u>

The word CONVERTED in English is not as good a translation as the words TURNED BACK—the Holman, NIV, and the Amplified all use TURNED BACK. When you are born again, your spirit man has become a new person, legally. Your spirit man is just as new as you were when you were born into this world, but it is through "the word of God" that you will save your soul or restore it. Paul compares the church to a marriage, that is cleansed by the washing of the water of the word of God. As we study the word and allow it to feed our minds, it feeds and changes our soul man, because truly "you are what you eat". Both in the natural and in the spiritual—proven so by science.

Let me share with you the method that God has chosen to feed us and change us into the person He wants us and called us to be.

The bible often speaks about marriage in connection to things done in the spirit; it does that to help us understand the principles of why we are asked to do certain things, *because we can often see these things in a marriage.*

In the letter to the church at Ephesus, Paul is giving the church the order of how men and women are to relate to each other, and in these scriptures, how they are both to relate to Christ.

Ephesians 5:25-27 NIV (commentary added)

> [25]Husbands, love your wives, just as Christ loved the church and gave himself up for her [26]to make her holy [separated from the world, hagiazo: to make clean, or render pure; set apart] cleansing her by the washing with water through the word, [27]and to present her to himself as a radiant church, without stain or wrinkle or any other blemish, but holy and blameless.
>
> *[cleansing comes from the word of God, which is how our soul becomes clean; through which we are washed and separated from the world]*

Our soulish man has not been regenerated yet. He still thinks like the world. This is what Jesus said to Peter, "You are with Me now, but you need to change, to stay with Me."

James 1:21 (KJV) James is speaking to believers; Christians he is presbyter over.

> [21]Wherefore lay apart all filthiness and superfluity of naughtiness, and receive with meekness the engrafted word, which is able to save your souls.

Receive with meekness the engrafted word, which is able to save your souls. James is speaking to born-again believers James wrote that, "it is the WORD of God that we implant in our soul; our mind, will and emotions that will save our soul from the devil and hell". Another word for word is seed. Receive the seed and let it grow. The engrafted word Comes from the Greek word, *EMPHUTOS,* which means to implant, causing to germinate or to spring up and produce a harvest. The harvest we are expecting is the person who planted—*emphutos,* the WORD, which is the seed they planted within themselves.

1 John 3:9 ESV

> ⁹No one born of God makes a practice of sinning, for God's seed abides in him; And he cannot keep sinning, because he has been born of God.

How sad that today too many are hearing 'God loves you and He knows you are not perfect, so do not worry that you are not always keeping from sin. If that is true as it is stated, then why did God say, 'be perfect as I am perfect?'

Matthew 5:48 HCSB

> ⁴⁸Be perfect, therefore, as your heavenly Father is perfect.

James 1:21 NIV

> ²¹Therefore, get rid of all moral filth and the evil that is so prevalent and humbly accept the word planted in you, which can save you.

You become the harvest; the first fruits of those who will do as you did, whom you will bring into the body of Christ.

James 1:21 AMPC

> ²¹So get rid of all uncleanness and the rampant outgrowth of wickedness, and in a humble (gentle, modest) spirit receive and welcome the Word which implanted and rooted [in your hearts] contains the power to save your souls.

What did James just say about the word? What did James say the word contains? The power to save your souls

I do not know how much planer James can make that for the reader or listener. It will take the word to change and save your soul, which is your mind, will, emotions. We cannot do that without Holy Spirit and any who think they can have not yet really tried to become what and who we must become. In the Greek, it is a picture of being born from another source [James 1:21] the gospel is represented here as being encompassed, or better said, wrapped up in the figure of a seed, or a shoot that has been implanted or engrafted, and is shown in Mark 4 as seed sown or seed being planted.

When something is engrafted, it has become one with its host, and the only way to separate it is by force, and by cutting it away from the source, which will cause the thing that is cut away to die.

Mark 4:14-15 HCSB

> ¹⁴The sower sows the word. ¹⁵These are the ones along the path where the word is sown: when they hear, immediately Satan comes and takes away the word sown in them.

This scripture tells the reader, or the listener, that when a person HEARS the WORD, it is so important and powerful, that satan comes immediately to take away the word, because he knows that if the word gets implanted or engrafted or sown correctly in you, it will establish a believer he will soon have to contend with in battle, and if he can remove the word of God in you, you will not be saved. He tries to stop it before the seed is planted, by planting in your minds what he wants you to think and believe, especially, since he has been practicing on you from the time you were born, He works, to remove faith, by planting doubt—that is what he did to Eve, and his methods have not changed, since the beginning of time up until now.

From that time to this, many have changed the Gospel from he came to save us from our sins, to, "he came to get us out of our troubles." And that is not true!!! So now for many who are taught this foolishness, instead of behaving like Jesus, we work at trying to make our Christianity work. That is so futile, and yet that is the predominate method the church uses today and it is failing, because its body members are failing, and are so like the world, there is no reason for the world to change, because the world can see that. Some are trying to make their denomination or religion work. That is not how His love works in us or for us.

1 John 4:16-17 NIV

> [16]And so we know and rely on the love God has for us.
> God is love. Whoever lives in love, lives in God, and God in them. [17]This is how love is made complete among us so that we will have confidence on the day of judgment: In this world we are like Jesus.

The word as or like is kathos in Greek; meaning equivalent to or likewise. Which one is it? Have we been converted or have we been reborn? **Have we been acting**, or are we as John just said? **That in this world we are like Jesus.**

Revivalist, Major Ian Thomas said, *"to be in Christ—that is redemption, but for Christ to be in you—that is sanctification. To be in Christ—that makes you fit for heaven, but for Christ to be in you—that makes you fit for earth. To be in Christ—that changes your destination, but for Christ to be in you—that changes your destiny. One makes heaven your home—the other makes the world His workshop."*

Some people are set free at the time of conversion, but many still carry in the soul and their flesh a great deal of conflict, even though they are free in their spirit. Others, because of very poor choices and an un-regenerated lifestyle and thought life, go back to the swallow they have come from, and take up the old habits. And truly for them, their life situation is now far worse than before, because they have given the enemy a place, a foothold, a stronghold. They are now, no longer happy in either place, nor will they ever be again.

They have never really left the prison their body and soul were in, because they have not changed their mindset or their friends or the places they go or the things they listen to or watch.

Galatians 4:9 (HCSB) Paul is speaking to believers in Christ, *[9]But now, since you know God, or rather have become known by*

God, how can you turn back again to the weak and bankrupt elemental forces? Do you want to be enslaved to them all over again? [Paul says in verse 9 these people are known by God]

Paul is asking the Galatian church, "do you wish to be enslaved again to what you have been set free from"? These people are born-again, but not going to heaven unless they change. Is it our relationship with Jesus that we are trying to make work? Or is it our denomination or religion we are trying to make work? Or perhaps it's the stuff we want people to see, so that they will believe we are someone and something we really aren't. Jesus, according to the word, NEVER saved a religion, denomination or any other institution, Jesus ONLY saves individual people.

And in Matthew 7 we read that many will think they are saved, like these people Paul has addressed in the church in Galatia, **because they have been working in the kingdom, but Jesus will TELL THEM, to go away,** because they never really had a relationship with Him, they only knew about Him **and about His own words, HE did not know them intimately.**

Matthew 7:22-23 HCSB

> [22]On that day many will say to Me, 'Lord, Lord, didn't we prophesy in Your name, drive out demons in Your name, and do many miracles in Your name?'
>
> [23]Then I will announce to them, 'I never knew you! Depart from Me, you lawbreakers!'

Most often the problem is the lack of word in us. We want a change of conditions, we want it our way, and without realizing it, we confuse the light, and the shadow, and the source, who is Jesus, with what we want. Jesus came to bring us the light—the truth. He was the shadow of things yet to come—He has come; there is no more shadow. The source is Jesus—all things were made by Him, and without Him was nothing made that was made. We often pray, Father, in the name of Jesus change this situation for me.

Paul asked the Father three times to remove the evil messenger sent from satan. The Father said to Paul the apostle three times, YOU DO IT.

Let's look at two great men in the bible who did as Paul did, they too asked God to do what God had commissioned them to do. They did not see or know whom they had become, now that

God was working in them, and it took a confrontation with life before they came to realize who they had become in God. Moses was told not to beg and Joshua was told to stop whining and praying. Moses is facing the Red Sea, with the entire Egyptian army behind him and no way out of the impending death, when the army arrives at his location. Moses is on the high precipice crying out to God to help them and God tells Moses to use what God has given him; to use the Rod of God, once called the staff of Moses. Moses lifted up the Rod and the sea parted and God did not need to do more for Moses than that; lesson learned.

Joshua was facing the army of his enemy and became full of fear and was whining before God, thinking he was praying, and God told him to get up and do what he already knew he was commissioned to do and stop praying for what God had already told him to do and given him authority and power to do; just like He has done to us, except we are not paying attention, because we, like Joshua, are functioning in fear and we see ourselves opposite the way that Christ sees us. Is our praying just like that of Joshua? Are we whining and complaining and in fear when we think we are praying? We spend too much time in our **head** *and not enough time in our heart.*

What do I mean by that?

Praying in the Spirit allows us to access heaven's understanding and it takes our heart to see what we do not always see with our head. It is from our heart that we engage with Holy Spirit. Our head has so much stuff aimed at it and so many sounds through media and other forms of communication that our minds become overwhelmed with worthless and needless information. And unfortunately, all of it has to be processed by our brain. This information is often no more than the opinions of others, but because we are finite beings, this information is heard and received and colors our spiritual thoughts with the world's opinions and those opinions are not eternal or helpful.

And more often than not, they do not happen as we were told they would and the end result is only to keep us off balance with needless and worthless opinions and ideas from the world, which is operating on behalf of the enemy of our souls, whose design is to steal from us the truth, take away our time and cause us loss and failure and misery. And today we are still asking the Father to remove certain problems or thorns.

The answer has not changed, He still says, "you do it."

Paraphrased; My grace was sufficient for Paul and it is sufficient for you. You speak to the situation, the condition, you do it in my name and the Father will, through Holy Spirit, back you up.

John 14:12-14 KJV (commentary added)

> ¹²Verily, verily, I say unto you, He that believeth on me, the works that I do shall he do also; and *greater works* than these shall he do; because I go unto my Father. *[greater works is the Greek word MEIZON, which means greater in number]*

> ¹³And whatsoever ye shall ask in my name, that will I do, that the Father may be glorified in the Son.

> ¹⁴If ye shall ask any thing in my name, I will do it.

John 15:14-16 KJV (commentary added)

> ¹⁴Ye are my friends, if ye do whatsoever I command you. *[in other words, if you do NOT do what He commands, you are not His friends]*

> ¹⁵Henceforth I call you not servants; for the servant knoweth not what his lord doeth: but I

have called you friends; for all things that I have heard of my Father I have made known unto you.

Read verse 15 again and see what Jesus has just told all of us.

Jesus said, that "everything I have heard from my Father I have told you", meaning that there is nothing that God has given Jesus that has not been made available to us.

> ¹⁶Ye have not chosen me, but I have chosen you, and ordained you, that ye should go and bring forth fruit, and that your fruit should remain: that whatsoever ye shall ask of the Father in my name, he may give it you.

After reading these verses, one can see that many of us are not hearing the voice of Christ, because we are overwhelmed with the words we are hearing from all the voices that are outside of Christ. We can only process so much, before our brain is overwhelmed with the world and its sound.

Matthew 10:7-8 (HCSB) Jesus said, *"⁷As you go, announce this: 'The kingdom of heaven has come near.' ⁸Heal the sick, raise the dead, cleanse those with skin diseases, drive out demons. You have received free of charge; give free of charge."*

I did not read here, where it says for us to pray and ASK God or Jesus. Jesus said 'heal the sick' that means we do what HE said to do.

For some reason, after we have read this scripture we turn around and pray—asking God to do what He told us to do. When the ten lepers came to Jesus, they asked him to heal them. What did he say? "Go show yourselves to the priests." Why did he say that? Because the Levitical law had already told the lepers how to get healing for leprosy. Jesus has just told them to do what they have already been told to do. The Bible records, "as they went, trusting in what Jesus said, they were healed." Where did they go? To the priests.

Jesus did not lay hands on them, he did not pray for them; he said by his actions, "I have obeyed the law and the commandments, now you go and you obey my commandment and you will get results too." When the lepers did what they were told to do by the Lord, they received their healing, and when we do what we are told to do by our Lord, we will receive what we have spoken—healing.

Where is the Kingdom of Heaven?

Jesus said the kingdom of heaven has come unto you. Jesus has told all of us that the kingdom of God has come to earth and Jesus brought it—that means it is here now, because He did not take it away from us.

Reading that and hearing that should encourage all of us to rethink our position in Christ, since we are not doing what we have been given to do, because we have not received into our hearts the magnitude of those words.

Matthew 12:28 (HCSB) Jesus confirms it again and again: *"If I drive out demons by the Spirit of God, then the kingdom of God has come to you."* Just because we profess to be born again doesn't mean we will enter into the kingdom of heaven. He that doeth the will of my Father will enter; obviously that means that whoever does NOT do the will of the Father will NOT enter—no matter what he or she professes, there are no other options.

Matthew 7:21 KJV

> [21]Not everyone that saith unto me, Lord, Lord, shall enter into the kingdom of heaven; but he that doeth the will of my Father which is in heaven.

Many profess to be born again, but they do not possess a relationship with the Savior, and more often than not—we know it, because we see and hear them. God, the Father resides in Heaven, the kingdom of heaven has come unto man and we are supposed to be the ones who reside here in that kingdom. These are two separate locations.

Psalm 115:16 HCSB

> [16]The heavens are the Lord's, but the earth He has given to the human race.

Matthew 7:22 KJV

> [22]Many will say to me in that day, Lord, Lord, have we not prophesied in thy name? and in thy name have cast out devils? and in thy name done many wonderful works?

Many will say, "prophesied in thy name." That is written as a question, **NOT a statement of fact.**

The word in Greek for have we not or didn't we is *ouk* [ouch] and means: *A full negation; it means NO or NOT; this word differs from the regular word used for not [we 3361], which is a word that implies a conditional and hypothetical negation; either yes or no.*

Listen carefully as I share what is actually being said here. The statement many will say is actually a question? Not a statement of fact. They were not sure if what they were speaking was from God. After all, this is the day of Judgment being discussed, and mere professors and not possessors will be judged and cast out. No more pretending to be a prophet or prophetic. No more games and no more pretenders of the faith.

Picture This Day with Me

Dancing around the issue of sold out to Christ is over; that is finished forever. The next statement made by them is also a question and then comes a statement, "in thy name cast out devils." The statement then says, and done many wonderful works. We have ALL assumed they are talking about healing and gifts of power. The people speaking are then told by Jesus, "depart you have worked evil". Look back at what they worked—they worked INIQUITY or evil. There was NO Holy Spirit POWER in evidence.

Since that is what Jesus said to them, what power did they work? They worked without knowing whose power they were using. Now watch this and catch the explanation of what I just said.

Matthew 7:22-26 NIV

> ²²Many will say to me on that day, 'Lord, Lord, did we not prophesy in your name and in your name drive out demons, and in your name perform many miracles?' ²³Then I will tell them plainly, 'I never knew you. Away from me, you evildoers!'

What were they doing and whose power were they using? Soulish or satanic? Here Jesus said what they did was evil, and He called them evil. God does NOT work evil. Meaning they belonged to the devil—even though they thought they were heaven bound and doing kingdom business. They were not in fellowship with Holy Spirit.

> ²⁴"Therefore everyone who hears these words of mine and puts them into practice is like a wise man who built his house on the rock. ²⁵The rain came down, the streams rose, and the winds blew and beat against that house; yet it did not fall, because it had its foundation on the rock. ²⁶But everyone who hears these words of mine and does not put them into practice is like a foolish man who built his house on sand."

There are more houses or lives being built on the sand than on the rock and it has begun to show, and the results of it have started to become very plain. The church in general is NOW nothing like God's plan from the beginning.

Read again *verse 26* and see that Jesus said that everyone who hears or reads what He has to say and does NOT do them is a fool and the foundation for his life is nothing more than sand; and sand cannot support the God life, it is not stable.

James 5:13-14 KJV in the early years of the church the disciples had a relationship with Christ and when they prayed for the sick the sick got healed.

> [13] Is any among you afflicted? let him pray. Is any merry? let him sing psalms.
>
> [14] Is any sick among you? let him call for the elders of the church; and let them pray over him, anointing him with oil in the name of the Lord:

Notice here that the expectation from anointing and prayer is healing and solution. Please also notice here that affliction and sickness are not the same.

- 2553 Afflicted—kakopatheo (kak-op-ath-eh'-o); to undergo hardship: be afflicted; To endure afflictions and hardship; to suffer trouble.
- 770 Sick is astheneo; without strength or power, weak and feeble; infirmity,

Not more than one generation passed before this verse and its requirements faded into 'last rites", which are the prayers prayed for those who are sick and soon to be departed from earth. The believers and the priests of the new generation did not have what all the disciples of the FIRST generation had, which was a relationship with Christ. Since there was no Godly presence or anointing when prayers were prayed, the recipient of the prayer usually died, so much of the time the prayer to heal the sick became known as the prayer of 'last rites', and was effete and irrelevant and worthless. Matthew 12:34-37 (HCSB) Jesus is speaking to Jews in leadership.

Priests who were in charge, but who had no relationship with God and did not know or understand His Presence, which made them ineffective and worthless. With each generation of believers something was lost and it appears that few even realized that what they had was nothing like the church was at the beginning. Here in this next exchange of Jesus with the

Jewish priests and leadership we see what Jesus thought about them.

> ³⁴Brood of vipers! How can you speak good things when you are evil? For the mouth speaks from the overflow of the heart. ³⁵A good man produces good things from his storeroom of good, and an evil man produces evil things from his storeroom of evil.
>
> [remember Matthew 7:22-23, on that day]
>
> ³⁶I tell you that on the day of judgment people will have to account for every careless word they speak.
>
> [careless means without profit—doubting words]

The original uses the word *IDLE* instead of careless—the meaning is the same. The original word is *ARGOS*, which means without effort; idle and inactive and not employed. The idea behind the word, when written in the bible, is slothful and lazy in Christian duty. We have a duty to use correct words—faith filled words, not insincere, false and unprofitable words. This also refers to the words of a person who speaks one thing and means another.

> ³⁷For by your words you will be acquitted, and
> by your words you will be condemned."

Jesus is speaking to the Jews, but He could be speaking to anybody and notice He does not say how can you, being evil speak good words. He said GOOD THINGS. He is speaking to men who have no well of life springing up in them; whose inside is evil. Void of a real relationship with Christ. There is no abundance of good in them. Since they have nothing inside of them to recall that is worth recalling, how can they speak good things? Things not words. Words produce things. Those of us who are not evil still fall under the same spiritual law—no water, no word in the well of our being—no well of life springing up. Either poor production or no production of things. Faith is the substance of things. Things are something you can see or touch

Hebrews 11:1 AMPC

> ¹Now faith is the assurance (the confirmation, the title deed) of the things [we] hope for, being the proof of things [we] do not see *and* the conviction of their reality [faith perceiving as real fact what is not revealed to the senses].

If we place our trust in Jesus—our faith in Him, our confidence in Him and we have His words inside of us, to the extent that they rise to the occasion first—then we, being good through Jesus, can speak good things. Things are substance. Words from you produce things. Things are healing; conditions changed and challenges met.

John 15:7 HCSB

> [7]If you remain in Me and My words remain in you, ask whatever you want and it will be done for you.

It would appear that many of us are not remaining in Christ and neither are His words, because Jesus said, from this place we can ask whatever we want and it will be done for us. It is necessary for us to see that Jesus has made it very plain in the word of God that if we comply with what is written in the word of God, we cannot fail and we will receive the desires of our hearts. This verse assures us that if the words Jesus has spoken and had written in His word are at home in us, when we use them, we will have what we asked. Words we say that Jesus said, words from His heart found in the word are SEEDS. Words are seeds, planted EVERY TIME WE OPEN OUR MOUTHS.

What are we saying? Are we claiming sicknesses as ours? Are we destroying our own potential with the words out of our own mouths? You can have what you say, especially what you say over and over again. Often when we are watching TV or listening to music we are saying without realizing it, what is being said or what is being sung in our minds, our subconscious. When we hear words, we say them to ourselves, because that is how we know what is being said or sung.

Think about that with me; we are rehearsing what is being said or sung, because that is how we understand and process. For instance, when I say apple, all of us picture an apple or if I say banana all of us picture a banana. When a song or commercial says something or shows something, we process that through our sub-conscience, and it stays there for 24 hours, until it is puffed out as hot air when we sleep, unless we think of it again or see it again or hear it again. When we hear something over and over again it begins to stick even though it was not our intention for that to happen. Hitler and other world leaders over the years have done that to persuade masses of people to think the way they want them to. Hearing the same commercial about a certain medication that does this or that, along with a witty or easy to remember jingle sets the thought in our minds, and we remember the song and without intending to, sometimes we even sing it. All because that is how we process information. Drug companies are keenly aware of this, and use it to create what is not even there, but becomes at home in us, because of its constant repetition.

Luke 11:2 HCSB

> ²He said to them, "Whenever you pray, say:
> Father, Your name be honored as holy. Your
> kingdom come.

Look at the word say—Jesus said, "when you pray, SAY"; too many are praying or saying what they are seeing or hearing, so that is what they are getting. There are many among us who are having repeat conversations about some subject, and that constantly saying of the subject is making it, the subject, plant itself, and after enough time, the saying it, brings it to life and now, 'it is so'. (See) 1 John 3:21, *If our heart does not condemn us we can have what we say...*

The positive side of this verse tells us that if we are in harmony and relationship with God, then our prayers or what we say, is what we can have. Are you aware that symptoms BEGIN AS nothing more than feelings? satan sends feelings or urges against us, to make us believe something that is not true, is true, UNTIL we claim or call or refer to the symptoms as ours. In the beginning of learning this truth it may take a while, but the more we live and repel him, and his lies, the more effective we become at sending the symptoms back to him.

CHAPTER TWO

Are you someone who is waiting for the right time?

You plan to commit to God and turn your life around, but not just yet. Perhaps you have accepted Jesus as Savior, but you are still Lord, and what you want to do, you do. There are things you want to do where God is not considered or given place by you. Consider this; Many have already missed the time, and others will miss the time of their visitation, and when the end comes for them, it will be too late.

Many of us are setting the stage for failure by the words we say consistently. The question that is most pressing for each of us is simply this; will I miss the time of my visitation? Will I miss my opportunity, because I did not realize this season is the season that God has planned to visit me? James tells us that we MUST be doers of the word, and not just those who hear and go away leaving what we heard on the floor, because what we heard, we allowed slip away, and we forgot what we heard. We did not realize that what we heard was revealing us, so we walked away after hearing only with our ears, and we missed the time of our visitation, our appointment with destiny—not just any destiny, but the destiny God had planned for us. How sad!

Hebrews 2:3 KJV

> ³How shall we escape, if we neglect so great salvation...

In other words, if we neglect this salvation there will be NO escape. He does not say, if we do not consider or if we reject it; he says neglect; He says NEGLECT and that means ignore, fail to consider, do not take seriously or behave as if it does not matter, because you have all the time in the world; or at least you think you do!!

How often today do we see people we once worshipped with staying away from church and appear not to be interested in attending any church anymore? What they are doing is NEGECTING this great salvation, and that is disobedience, just as if it was some sin that we consider a greater sin, because the word tells us very pointedly, "do not forget the assembling of yourselves together".

Hebrews 10:23–25 HCSB

> ²³Let us hold on to the confession of our hope without wavering, for He who promised is faithful. ²⁴And let us be concerned about one another in order to promote love and good

> works, ²⁵not staying away from our worship meetings, as some habitually do, but encouraging each other, and all the more as you see the day drawing near.

What is even sadder; most who go away as hearers only, miss not just the time of their visitation—they miss the plans and purposes that God has for them. They miss their destiny; a destiny that has been planned by God for them before they were ever born.

Jeremiah 29:11 HCSB

> 11 For I know the plans I have for you"—this is the Lord's declaration—"plans for your welfare, not for disaster, to give you a future and a hope."

The Lord has already made declarations over you. He has decreed what His plans are for you, BUT you did not watch and you did not listen, and you did not do what you were shown you must do—how sad. Scriptures declare that we cannot even imagine what God has prepared for us. None of it will matter to those who hear, and do NOT do, meaning put into practice what they heard. Why? Because, they are satisfied to be hearers only.

They choose to neglect this great salvation and leave God no choice but to turn them away from Him, and into everlasting destruction and separation from God. Hearers only, and disinterested people; those who have chosen to consider this salvation lightly and do not take what Jesus did seriously are those who put out little or no effort to grab hold of God. God's response to them will be as theirs was to Him. They will part from Him for eternity; their failure to hear and listen and obey has cost them eternity. The devil, satan, has outrun them; God is no longer in the picture only judgment and hell remains.

On the other hand, those who listen and obey will have blessing after blessing in this lifetime and a relationship with the One who created them to be victorious and overcome satan and all that he has thrown at them. Some people who consider themselves Christians are trying to remain close to the world. We know that by the decisions they make every day. The world is supposed to recognize the disciples of Jesus as His true children.

Jesus said, His disciples are not of this world. Yet the predominate number of people who claim Christianity are desperately trying to fit into the world. Peter told us to be peculiar people, and instead of that, many have become weird and absurd, and whose behavior borders on the ridiculous.

Peculiar here means to be special; in many ways, be active and performing and fulfilling and redeeming and insightful, excellent, honorable, purposeful, committed, and there are about 20 more words used to translate this word; *peripoiesis*. This is someone with a purpose and who produces success. So much for peculiar and behaving in foolishness and absurdity.

We are designed to have purpose and be a success. The greater number of people who attend church and claim Christ as Lord do not want to be seen in the light of what Christ has just said, because if they do, it will require from them a commitment to the Lord they are not willing to make. Not everyone wants to be insightful, excellent, honorable, purposeful.

Some of them have been trying to fit into the world their entire lives and yet their savior NEVER wanted them to fit in, He wanted them to "come out from the world and yet OCCUPY it at the same time." Occupy, meaning, 'do not become like the world—do not fit into the world. Be overcomers in the world and occupy or be in charge while you are here. Take a trip with me and together let's look at how our Savior intends for us to occupy and still not become overcome by the world.

Ephesians 3:20 HCSB

> ²⁰Now unto him that is able to do exceeding abundantly above all that we ask or think, according to the power that worketh in us,

WHERE IS THAT POWER WORKING? IN US. What do the words, according to mean? **They mean to come down from or down through.** It means that the measure of power in us is based on the relationship we have with Christ, and it comes down from or down through Him. Ephesians 4:7 (HCSB) says, *"Now grace was given to each one of us according to the measure of the Messiah's gift."*

This verse tells us that the gift or grace of God is distributed to us according to the measure or amount of Christ in us. Christ is God's word alive or living in us. Or said another way, Christ is the mind of God, expressed in words, incarnated in a human body and those words and Christ are the same, and they are the seed of the universe, dwelling in those who are redeemed. Let me reiterate once more that salvation according to James is our participation in using the WORD of God every day in our lives. James WROTE that the Word contains the power to save our soul, which means that those who fail to implant and root the

Word of God as a staple of everyday life are not doing what the believer is required to do to change their life.

James 1:21 AMPC

> ²¹So get rid of all uncleanness and the rampant outgrowth of wickedness, and in a humble (gentle, modest) spirit receive *and* welcome the Word which implanted *and* rooted [in your hearts] contains the power to save your souls.

The portion that has been measured off, the measure or limit or amount of Christ in us is dependent on us. God's words in us are seed and seeds grow.

John 15:7 KJV

> ⁷If ye abide in me, and my words abide in you, ye shall ask what ye will, and it shall be done unto you.

HIS WORDS ARE TO BE IN US and we are to abide and dwell in Him.

Ephesians 3:20 HCSB

> [20]Now to Him who is able to do above and beyond all that we ask or think according to the power that works in us.

Listen to how this reads when we combine the intention of verses Ephesians 4;7, John 15:7 and Ephesians 3:20. This is the intent of what was written, *"If you habitually stay in Christ and His words habitually stay or dwell in you, you shall ask what you will and He shall come down through you, according to the power of the word that works in you as a habit, as a lifestyle."*

Let me share with you what being habituated in Christ and having his word at home in you will do to propel you toward success in the kingdom of God. Read this next verse with me from two different translations of Proverbs.

Proverbs 20:27 KJV

> [27]The spirit of man is the candle of the LORD, searching all the inward parts of the belly.

Proverbs 20:27 HCSB

> [27]The Lord's lamp sheds light on a person's life, searching the innermost parts.

The word for lamp or candle that He uses here means more than a lamp or light or candle, as we understand the word today. The Lord's light is revealing and communicating spiritual truth. What does that mean? The candle of the Lord or the lamp of the Lord is the gleam in God's eye, as He is searching all the inward parts of our emotional hunger in the spirit looking for the basis of our understanding that He has placed in our spirit man. Why is He searching the belly? This is where He has located the soil of our spirit man, which has been tilled and where God sees the gleam of a fresh furrow. This picture in the spirit means this man is ready for God's seed to be planted. The word has the meaning of the hollow of the belly or the womb. This is the creative part of man and the area where both men and women create or destroy. This is the area of passion and compassion. We read in John what this will produce in us and others like us

John 7:38 HCSB

> 38The one who believes in Me, as the Scripture has said, will have streams of living water flow from deep within him.

That is not **maybe** or **could be,** it is **will be!** We have no power or authority outside of Christ.

Read that verse again SLOWLY and hear what is being said to us. If we do indeed believe in Jesus the Christ, we will have streams of living water flowing up from deep inside of us. How sad that as believers we almost never see that, either in ourselves or in other believers. Jesus said that the ONE WHO BELIEVES IN ME; the only exclusion is if we don't believe in Him. Jesus expects all believers to measure up to this verse or He never would have said it. It would appear to me, that we have no idea of what it really means to obey His word or to believe in Him. Jesus' total obedience to the Father is what brought his total victory. That is what conquered satan.

Ephesians 3:20 KJV

> [20]Now unto him that is able to do exceeding abundantly above all that we ask or think, according to the power that worketh in us.

Now we all still sin—some more and some less; it is not just the sin that keeps us away from His light as much as it is the failure to ask forgiveness and move back into God's grace that keeps us out of His light. Jesus has taken Peter, James and John to a high mountain where Jesus is transfigured before them. Transfiguration is the miracle of transformation from an earthly form into a supernatural form, which was seen and felt by the radiance of His garments and His visual appearance and countenance. Each one in that cloud was enclosed in light that none of the 3 apostles had ever seen.

Matthew 17:14-21 (RSV) in what we are about to read, Jesus and the three have come down from the mountain. They have left the light of the Transfiguration of Jesus and descended into the natural realm of the earth and here they are confronted by the crowd with the other 9 apostles who were not invited by Jesus to go up the mountain with Him.

> [14]When they came to the crowd, a man came to him, knelt before him, [15]and said, "Lord, have mercy on my son, for he is an epileptic and he suffers terribly; he often falls into the fire and often into the water. [16]And I brought him to your disciples, but they could not cure him." [17]Jesus answered, "You faithless and perverse generation, how much longer must I be with you? How much longer must I put up with you? Bring him here to me." [18]And Jesus rebuked the demon, and it came out of him, and the boy was cured instantly. [19]Then the disciples came to Jesus privately and said, "Why could we not cast it out?" [20]He said to them, "Because of your

> little faith. For truly I tell you, if you have faith the size of a mustard seed, you will say to this mountain, 'Move from here to there,' and it will move; and nothing will be impossible for you."

This has nothing to do with the size of the mustard seed—this is to reveal how small an amount of faith it takes to manifest results. Again, it is not the size of the seed, but how little genuine faith it takes to move the mountains in our lives. Jesus is carrying the light of Transfiguration and He is full of the light that covered and transformed Him, and says to them:

Matthew 17:21 KJV

> [21]Howbeit this kind goeth not out but by prayer and fasting.

Jesus is talking about a lifestyle—it is fine to fast for three days in January to start the year, but here, Jesus is talking about a fasted life. The reason we live a fasted life is keep our flesh under control, which gives us power over the devil and his minions. There are different devils and different levels of power. There are different levels of intelligence and power in the spirit realm, and these levels operate as an army with the stronger and more intelligent in command. You will notice that

if you are reading the NIV or the RSV verse 21 does not appear—
When Verse 21 is written it says;

> [21]Howbeit this kind goeth not out but by prayer and fasting. (KJV)

It always makes sense to read several different translations of the bible, that way you will be able to pick up a better understanding of what the word says. The fallen angels have been given authority over the ethnic groups and nations and cities and world-wide leaders and under them is a hierarchy of demons with from great, to very little power. Matthew 17:18 (NIV) we see an example of this in this account of the boy, *"Jesus rebuked the demon, and it came out of the boy, and he was healed at that moment."*

> [SPIRIT: In verse 18 the word devil or demon is pneuma, the one Jesus rebuked. 4151 pneuma- has positive meanings and negative, here it is negative. A spirit is a simple essence]

A demon or spirit is a creation having NO physical presence, and possessed of the power of knowing, desiring, deciding, and acting. Here the word is used for demons, or evil spirits, who inhabited the bodies of men The fact that these disciples could operate as effectively as they did against demons, was because of the presence of Jesus. His presence was the substance of their faith.

We have others during the time of Jesus who did not know Jesus, but heard about the power of His name and tried to use what they had no right to use and it cost them.

Acts 19:13–15 NIV

> ¹³Some Jews who went around driving out evil spirits tried to invoke the name of the Lord Jesus over those who were demon-possessed.

They would say, "In the name of the Jesus whom Paul preaches, I command you to come out."

> ¹⁴Seven sons of Sceva, a Jewish chief priest, were doing this. ¹⁵One day the evil spirit answered them, "Jesus I know, and Paul I know about, but who are you?"

They were using the name of Jesus as the weapon against the demons—it did not work for them, because they had no relationship with Jesus. His presence was not with them.

After reading verse 15, it could be that early on, the disciples had success, however, one day, the evil spirit stopped them to address who they really were, because Jesus was nowhere near them, and the demons could FEEL His absence.

Back to the 7 sons of Sceva.

> [15]One day the evil spirit answered them, "Jesus I know, and Paul I know about, but who are you?"

Even though the word know is written as know two times side by side, they each have a different meaning. The 1st I know is the word ginosko, which translates as, I feel His presence, I sense Him nearby. That is the meaning of the word, know, that is 1st expressed in verse 15. The second time the word know appears, it is the word, *epistamahee*, which means, I am aware of him, he comes to mind.

The NIV does a good job of translating this second "I KNOW," and says, "I know about him," and so does the HCSB, which says "I recognize Paul", but some translations do not translate it as accurately as they should. There should be a difference in what demons recognize and know about our Christ and any of us. The spirits could feel the presence of Jesus, they could sense Him nearby, even though He might not be in the immediate area.

When the demons said they KNOW HIM, they were saying we not only know who He is, but we feel His very presence somewhere close.

In Paul's case, evil spirits knew who he was, and they also knew that Holy Spirit was with him, and he possessed the goods to make them leave, even though he was not Jesus—they still knew him, but they did not have any real knowledge about these alleged exorcists, who were sons of Sceva, who knew ABOUT Jesus, but did not have a personal relationship with Him. The sons of Sceva were attempting to use the name of someone without his authorization. They ONLY knew about this Jesus, they did not know Him, there was no personal connection, and Jesus did not know them personally, so this password "in the name of Jesus"] did not work for them

In modern terms they were trying to access an account they were not authorized to access, or use a credit card that was not theirs. The disciples of Jesus were operating in the authority of Jesus with his knowledge and permission. The 7 sons of Sceva did not have the authority of Jesus behind them or their words. Today we are supposed to operate in His authority WITH His knowledge and permission and He is to reside in us as the presence of Holy Spirit.

In Matthew 10:1 (HCSB) read with me a case of that authority in practice.

> ¹Summoning His 12 disciples, He gave them authority over unclean spirits, to drive them out and to heal every disease and sickness.
>
> [*naos; nosos,* sick or sickness refers to disease in this verse. Sickness in this verse is the word *malakia*, which means queer; sexual behavior contrary to nature.]

CHAPTER THREE

When Jesus was leaving the temple where He had been teaching by example how faith operates, he said to the two blind men who were following Him, "according to your faith be it so unto you." That statement "according to your faith be it so unto you "applies to the disciples also, and was said in their presence. The following is the account of Jesus teaching these two men.

According to Your Faith

Matthew 9:28–29 HCSB

> [28]When He entered the house, the blind men approached Him, and Jesus said to them, "Do you believe that I can do this?" "Yes, Lord," they answered Him. [29]Then He touched their eyes, saying, "Let it be done for you according to your faith!"

The disciples were watching Jesus in operation; they too could only operate according to their level of faith. After this, the people brought a man possessed with a dumb or mute spirit so that Jesus could heal him.

Matthew 9:32–33 NIV

> ³²While they were going out, a man who was demon-possessed and could not talk was brought to Jesus. ³³And when the demon was driven out, the man who had been mute spoke.

The crowd was amazed and said, "Nothing like this has ever been seen in Israel." When we study the scripture, we see that blind, deaf and dumb spirits appear to have a level of authority and power that is higher than the demons of many other infirmities. Not everyone can make them leave. The reason for that is light. When any previous exorcist cast out a demon, it was of a lower intelligence and power level. We see the seven sons of Sceva as an example; they had been casting out low-level demons, until a demon of a higher level of authority challenged them. No one could ever do what Jesus had done, because no one had His level of light.

John 1:1-9 KJV

> 1In the beginning was the Word, and the Word was with God, and the Word was God.
>
> ²The same was in the beginning with God.

³All things were made by him; and without him was not any thing made that was made.

⁴In him was life; and the life was the light of men.

⁵And the light shineth in darkness; and the darkness comprehended it not.

⁶There was a man sent from God, whose name was John.

⁷The same came for a witness, to bear witness of the Light, that all men through him might believe.

⁸He was not that Light, but was sent to bear witness of that Light.

⁹That was the true Light, which lighteth every man that cometh into the world. Which lighteth, means to give understanding]

[LIGHT: *PHOS*-- The power of understanding of moral and spiritual truth.]

Jesus brought that. It is part of the kingdom of God that Jesus brought here to planet earth.

> [DARKNESS: 4653 *skotia* - SKO-TIA 3)
> metaphorically, used of ignorance of divine
> things, and its associated wickedness]

In the verses we just read, the word Darkness refers to ignorance of divine things and it is associated with wickedness and the resultant misery in hell. That verse is saying 'No one just dies—in death there is always a reward—the wages of sin is death AND IN DEATH comes the misery of hell or the Glory of heaven—ALWAYS.' Jesus LIGHTETH every man:5461 *photizo*-3) to bring to light, to make something evident; to cause something to exist and thus come to light and to become clear to all. Paul in Romans 1:18-25 says the same thing. In John 1:9 it means to give understanding to. And which lighteth means to give understanding to those without understanding.

John 1:10–17 HCSB

> [10] He was in the world,
> and the world was created through Him,
> yet the world did not recognize Him.

[11]He came to His own,
and His own people did not receive Him.

[12]But to all who did receive Him,
He gave them the right to be children of God,
to those who believe in His name,

[13]who were born,
not of blood,
or of the will of the flesh,
or of the will of man,
but of God.

[14]The Word became flesh
and took up residence among us.
We observed His glory, the glory
 as the One and Only Son from the Father,
full of grace and truth.

[15](John testified concerning Him and exclaimed,
"This was the One of whom I said,
'The One coming after me has surpassed me,
 because He existed before me.'")

[16]Indeed, we have all received grace after grace
 from His fullness,

> ¹⁷for the law was given through Moses,
> grace and truth came through Jesus Christ.

READ verse 17 one more time.

> ¹⁷for the law was given through Moses,
> grace and truth came through Jesus Christ.

In my understanding, grace is a power of God given unto men to do the will of God. Please notice that grace and truth came when Jesus came. Prior to Jesus, we had covenant and Abraham is one recorded to have had faith as well as covenant. A number of the Old Testament patriarchs were said to have operated out of faith; Able, Enoch, Noah, Abraham, Sarah, Isaac Jacob, Joseph, Moses and even Rahab, BUT David is said to have operated out of covenant.

The others we have not listed were recorded as having understood their covenant with God or having heard Him speak to them and operated out of a covenant relationship. They did not function by faith, but out of covenant relationship. Whether we think we operate out of faith or the New Covenant, please notice one thing that all of them held in common. ACTION, and accomplishment. Is that how God sees me? full of action and accomplishment.

Jesus said to His disciples "occupy until I come back". Jesus spoke a faith filled word—occupy—that is an action word—a word of function and accomplishment. A word of construction and building. Jesus is teaching His disciples and, as was His method, He uses a parable to explain the position of the kingdom of heaven that has come to earth. Let me briefly reintroduce the parable again using two different translations.

Luke 19:12–13 KJV

> ¹²Jesus said therefore, A certain nobleman went into a far country to receive for himself a kingdom, and to return.
>
> ¹³And he called his ten servants, and delivered them ten pounds, and said unto them, Occupy till I come.
>
> *[This royal power is not to be confused with an actual kingdom, but the right or authority to rule over a kingdom.]*

In other words; run the business until I come back. And let's look at the NIV, which further explains what Christ was saying.

> [12]He said: "A man of noble birth went to a distant country to have himself appointed king and then to return. [13]So he called ten of his servants and gave them ten minas. 'Put this money to work,' he said, 'until I come back.'

The nobleman gave his servants the tools to function in his absence, THEN he said, occupy, which is the word the King James uses. The Lord or master gave servants what was necessary to accomplish the goals he set for them and his business. They all knew how the master functioned and knew what he expected when he returned from his journey.

Allow me to tell you my definition of faith; "faith is using common sense, by doing the right thing at the right time, and resting assured that it was the right thing, and having an expectation it will turn out in your favor, because it was based upon the WORD of God".

Faith is function WITH expectation and that is how it was, and still is today in the kingdom of heaven, and Jesus said, "The kingdom of heaven has come to earth" Faith is function with expectation. Faith was designed by God to be common sense, but today it is NOT so common.

Luke 1:1-2 NIV

> ¹Many have undertaken to draw up an account of the things that have been fulfilled among us, ²just as they were handed down to us by those who from the first were eyewitnesses and servants of the word.

The word that Luke uses here for things is *PRAGMA*, meaning the things or matters of law that are being accomplished. Matters of law are what Jesus came to do and we are to do too. It is the same word that is used for OCCUPY.

In verse 2 it says, "these things were handed down to us, by servants of the word of God." What things is he talking about? The things that we have read here are the same things that Jesus came to earth to be Lord over and these things in Greek are the word *PRAGMA*. Meaning, the matters at law as well as other things that are being accomplished. The disciples, previous to Jesus, were not exorcists, but now they were suddenly given power to exorcise demons and evil spirits. Out they went with this new fire, like new converts ready for all comers and they were successful and they won and they beat back the enemy. Taking back the world from the enemy is a matter of law. They went out in covenant relationship and obedience but NOT

FAITH. Time passed by and time can do two things, increase growth or decay.

At this point they still had Jesus with them and their confidence was that He was nearby, so they functioned as He told them to function, but with little faith, as He said in Matthew 17:20, just after He said, "they were a faithless and perverse generation". And these are included in the things that Jesus came to be Lord over, and Jesus came to make us lord over. The word, occupy, and the word things are the same word, *PRAGMA*.

Why this lengthy discussion of these two words? It is apparent the church in general does not have a grasp on the word faith and uses it way beneath the biblical intention of the bible authors and therefore God. Jesus said, "occupy" to his disciples. The word in ENGLISH that means occupy is PRAGMATIC; practical, sensible. It means that we should be busy, and active and have strong opinions. A pragmatic person is one who has oriented themselves towards the success of a specific line of action. We were told when we began our new life in Christ to be peculiar people. But no one told us what peculiar means, especially those of us who are seeking after God with all our hearts.

Please let me share with you what PECULIAR means here. Jesus said, orient yourselves towards the success of the kingdom of heaven that has come down to earth—that is your assignment and the function of that assignment is your destiny as My children and friends and servants.

It is also apparent that we have read over the word things, as just another word, to get us to the next word in the verse, and that has caused us great loss in what the kingdom is all about, and who we are in this kingdom that has come to earth. When we occupy, we are going about in faith, doing the things of the kingdom just as Jesus would have done.

John 7:38 HCSB

> [38]The one who believes in Me, as the Scripture has said, will have streams of living water flow from deep within him."

Some translations say streams and some say *rivers of living water.* Is this about me? Am I this person? I want to see this in me and in you.

John 7:39 HCSB

> ³⁹He said this about the Spirit. Those who believed in Jesus were going to receive the Spirit, for the Spirit had not yet been received because Jesus had not yet been glorified/resurrected.

He that believeth on me, out from his womb, out of the creative center of his spirit man shall flow rivers of living water. [OF LIVING *ZAO*]. The word for water lends itself to the idea of abundance of water and it comes from the base word that means rain. [*HUDOS*, or *HUDATOS*]

> [2198 *ZAO*—living, having vital power in itself and exerting the same power.]

Out of the belly, the creative center of man's spirit, shall flow vital power and it will exert that power upon the mind, will and emotion. The word for believeth is *PISTEUO*: to have faith, to put confidence in, to put trust in.

Now let me translate John 7:38 which we just read, *He that puts his confidence and trust in me, from the creative center of his being, shall come out powerful floods and vigorous rains that changes lives.*

This is life-giving power that is able to produce the result we want through the flow out of him and into us of Holy Spirit. We have no power or authority outside of Christ. Jesus' total obedience to the Father is what brought his total victory. That is what conquered satan. Jesus must be the substance of our faith, because in and through us, Jesus said we conquer satan as Jesus would if He were here. His presence is the substance of our faith and His presence is Holy Spirit in us.

Jesus said to His own disciples; they were a part of a wicked and perverse generation, and then He said they had little faith? Why did He say that? Because they could only operate under His authority, since up to this point they had not yet moved into faith. They were operating out of covenant and obedience and as the demons said—we feel Jesus—we sense His presence nearby—we ginosko—know Him.

The demons said, "Jesus, I know and Paul I am aware of"—they did not say that about the disciples, because they did not yet operate in faith. It is His presence in us that gives us faith. His presence is the substance of our faith.

The next thing is his power over evil, which must become a part of us based upon our lifestyle. The light that emanated from his spirit man could actually be recognized from a distance, by the demons. It must become so visible, that demons seeing Jesus or Paul would recognize that same power in me or in you. When Peter in his later years walked by the sick and they were healed; it was the light that emanated from His spirit that brought healing and that light is the Spirit of God in our inner man, our belly man. The area of our spirit man that creates or destroys. The more of him and the less of us will display a greater level of light.

Jesus must become the substance of our faith and faith is action + function.

CHAPTER FOUR

Jesus left us to gain the kingdom; when He left, He left us with spiritual gifts to do the job that was required of us. He gave us the authority and right that He gained to function and operate through us, as if He never left, which is available to each one of us who are redeemed. Jesus gave us faith and told us to function.

Mark 3:7–12 (ESV) before we read these verses recall with me that Jesus and His disciples are in the temple and Jesus heals the man with a withered hand and after Jesus healed that man, the Pharisees and Herodians started to plan how they could destroy Jesus.

> 7Jesus withdrew with his disciples to the sea, and a great crowd followed, from Galilee and Judea 8and Jerusalem and Idumea and from beyond the Jordan and from around Tyre and Sidon. When the great crowd heard all that he was doing, they came to him. 9And he told his disciples to have a boat ready for him because of the crowd, lest they crush him, 10for he had healed many, so that all who had diseases

pressed around him to touch him. ¹¹And whenever the unclean spirits saw him, they fell down before him and cried out, "You are the Son of God." ¹²And he strictly ordered them not to make him known.

The original writing is much clearer in its meaning. Listen to a better way to have translated this, based on how it was originally written. And the unclean spirits, whenever they would see Jesus, fell down before Him and yelled, saying, Thou art the Son of God! And He kept rebuking them severely, because He did want them to make Him known to the public. It is from here that Jesus went to a mountain to pray and He prayed all night according to Luke 7:12. In the morning Jesus called His disciples and chose 12 whom He named apostles. Then Jesus and His apostles came down from the mountain, where they were met by a great crowd of people.

It is here that Jesus healed all who were sick and delivered all who were demonized and it is from here at this time that Jesus gave us the Beatitudes. Healing the man with the withered hand in the temple gave Jesus notoriety and acclaim and up to this point in time no such thing had ever been done, so to say that the people were interested in seeing and hearing this Jesus is an understatement. Luke 8:22–25 (ESV) after healing all the sick and demonized that came to him, Jesus and His apostles left Galilee and went to Judea.

> ²²One day he got into a boat with his disciples, and he said to them, "Let us go across to the other side of the lake." So, they set out, ²³and as they sailed he fell asleep. And a windstorm came down on the lake, and they were filling with water and were in danger. ²⁴And they went and woke him, saying, "Master, Master, we are perishing!"

And he awoke and rebuked the wind and the raging waves, and they ceased, and there was a calm.

> ²⁵He said to them, "Where is your faith?" And they were afraid, and they marveled, saying to one another, "Who then is this, that he commands even winds and water, and they obey him?"

Think with me for a moment: *A number of these men who are with Jesus on this boat are expert sailors and knew how to handle a boat in bad weather; Jesus is a carpenter, so how can a carpenter help them in this storm?* This storm forces them to face the fact that they can no longer help themselves and that indeed they had no faith. Prior to this they always had a way out of whatever they were in, but now their very lives were in jeopardy, and there is no way out of it. They did not consider that Jesus had never sailed a boat; they were forced to abandon their own resources and strength and call upon the only one they knew who had influence with God.

Luke 8:25 ESV

> [25]He said to them, "Where is your faith?" And they were afraid, and they marveled, saying to one another, "Who then is this, that he commands even winds and water, and they obey him?"

We shared that having faith in God, Jesus and Holy Spirit is using common sense. Our spirit man is using common sense when he exercises his faith. Because if we can believe for all the things that have been created to be where we left them when we get up from the night, or go someplace, then maybe it is time to believe and trust and have confidence in the one who put them there. The disciples had knowledge that Jesus had influence with God and since we know that Jesus said that, RECALL He also said as He was, so are we; now it will be up to us to do what

Jesus said we had the authority and power to take dominion over all the earth and occupy and direct the world to obey the words of God.

Genesis 1:26 ESV

> [26]Then God said, "Let us make man in our image, after our likeness. And let them have dominion over the fish of the sea and over the birds of the heavens and over the livestock and over all the earth and over every creeping thing that creeps on the earth."

Genesis 1:28 ESV

> [28]And God blessed them. And God said to them, "Be fruitful and multiply and fill the earth and subdue it, and have dominion over the fish of the sea and over the birds of the heavens and over every living thing that moves on the earth."

The redeemed are supposed to be using the laws of God to take back what the devil has stolen and do the things that Jesus came to do when He was here. The disciples have exposed to the SPIRIT WORLD that they were not as Jesus was. The spirits DID

NOT KNOW THAT ABOUT THEM AT FIRST. In the beginning the evil spirits were confused, everything that was happening was happening so fast and was so new, and had never happened before, and now that Jesus had come to earth, it was all happening too fast and they were reeling from the effects of it. In what we have just read, YOU will notice that Jesus **did not pray.** He gave a command and the storm ceased.

Jesus prayed early and late and on some occasions all night. His life was one of fasting and prayer—He began His walk by fasting and praying for 40 days. During the times when He was not in His prayer closet, He more often gave a command or spoke a word. Jesus by example, is showing us there are times to pray and times to command. We pray through in our prayer closet, but when we come out to do battle, we give the word of creation that has been birthed in our belly from our personal time of being in the secret place with God. Intercession is NOT something we do in public, any more than giving birth is a public event.

We have become so conditioned to doing what we have always done, that to make an appropriate change is still difficult for many of us. We often pray, when we should be commanding and proclaiming and decreeing in bold faith. I hear People say; 'I did that, or I used to do that, and nothing happened'—well do it again, until something does happen. How on earth will we test our faith unless we put it on the line?

Luke 8:26–27 ESV

Then they— [Jesus and His disciples]

> [26]Then they sailed to the country of the Gerasenes, which is opposite Galilee. [27]When Jesus had stepped out on land, there met him a man from the city who had demons. For a long time, he had worn no clothes, and he had not lived in a house but among the tombs.

If you are reading this account in the synoptic gospels, which are Matthew, Mark, or Luke, you will notice there appears to be some differences. By the way, synoptic means similar, that is why the three are called the synoptic gospels, because they are similar, not exact, but similar. Why isn't John a synoptic gospel? Because it covers a different period of time, and it focuses heavily on the ministry of Jesus in Judea. Matthew records that there were 2 demoniacs. Mark and Luke infer that there was only one. Matthew says this occurred in the land of the Gadarenes, which is a town near the lake where this occurred. Mark and Luke say it was the land of Gerasenes. Both names refer to two cities located near the lake and neither of the names or the location have any bearing on the actual event that occurred near that lake. According to Matthew 8:28 when others stepped foot on shore he was so violent that no one could pass that way.

What propelled him to run to the beach and fall on his knees? HE SAW A GREAT LIGHT.

Luke 8:28 ESV

> [28]When he saw Jesus, he cried out and fell down before him and said with a loud voice, "What have you to do with me, Jesus, Son of the Most High God? I beg you, do not torment me."

Some commentaries and bibles say that the demon possessed man fell down at Jesus' feet in worship, but the text does not support that thinking. Most likely he was drawn to the light of Jesus and was fearful of His power, and as his conversation says, 'are you here to begin our torment?' Matthew says, 'torment us before the time'.

When the demon possessed man said, 'son of God the most high', it was not worship, but the acknowledgment that Jesus was God, and indeed the epithet, or name, 'Son of the most high

God,' was how he and all the demon possessed addressed Jesus. The spirits controlling the man saw the light from Jesus. Please note that the disciples were with Him, but the only one the demon possessed man noticed, was JESUS.

Luke 8:28-31 KJV

> [28]When he saw Jesus, he cried out, and fell down before him, and with a loud voice said, What have I to do with thee, Jesus, thou Son of God most high? I beseech thee, torment me not.
>
> [29](For he had commanded the unclean spirit to come out of the man. For oftentimes it had caught him: and he was kept bound with chains and in fetters; and he broke the bands, and was driven of the devil into the wilderness.)
>
> [30]And Jesus asked him, saying, What is thy name? And he said, Legion: because many devils were entered into him.
>
> [31]And they besought him that he would not command them to go out into the deep.

This word deep has nothing to do with the sea or water or lake or any such thing. [the Greek word here for deep is {ABUSSOS} the abyss or the bottomless pit]

Luke 8:32–33 ESV

> [32]Now a large herd of pigs was feeding there on the hillside, and they begged him to let them enter these. So, he gave them permission. [33]Then the demons came out of the man and entered the pigs, and the herd rushed down the steep bank into the lake and drowned.

In Mark 5:6 we see this man ran to Jesus when he saw Him afar off and some translators said, "he worshipped Him". Matthew gives an incomplete account of this occurrence and it is very likely that he was not present when this occurred, and why he alone, says that there were two men who were possessed, and why he alone mentions a different city.

When we read the book of Matthew the account of the demoniac occurs in chapter 8 of his book and then in chapter 9, Matthew records that Jesus calls Matthew to follow him. If Matthew is recording this chronologically, then he is telling what he remembers of what he was told about this, and not what he personally saw. We all know that Matthew was last to join Jesus, and became the 12th Apostle.

The spirit controlling the man recognized the light in Jesus- causing the man he possessed to run to Jesus in fear and begged Jesus to send them into the swine. The demons begged through this demonic principality to be placed into the pigs. That means they could not go without Jesus' permission.

Demons do not want to go into DRY PLACES to wander, because they cannot express themselves in dry places like they can in human or animal forms. Humans and animals are 87 % water and allow demons a place of the expression of their personalities. A dry place is a place where there is no live flesh. Demons want to be housed in flesh, preferably human flesh.

Mark records that there were about two thousand pigs. Luke, who was present, says that there were many swine, with no specific number being counted. Pigs know how to swim—and since that is the case, why did they drown? The demons drowned the pigs, because they did NOT want to express themselves through pigs—or, could it be that the pigs would rather die than let demons control them?

This leader of thousands of demons was not a lower-level spirit, he was a principality and he wanted a person or people for his place of expression and he wanted to keep his army of demons under his charge in this territory. And consider with me that when someone other than Jesus came to shore, he attacked them, so he was the principality or the one who controlled this land of 10 cities, known as the Decapolis. He not only had a preference for where he would go, he also wanted to stay in the area—he had a preference for this area, just like we do for our nation or our homeland. This gives us ample evidence that he was of a much higher level of authority and intelligence in the spirit world. This also gives rise to the fact that he was a principality over this territory where they had come on shore. Demons are disembodied spirits; meaning without a body for expression.

The demon principality was afraid that he and his cohorts would be cast into hell or into dry places before their time. He asked for indwelling into the pigs—he knew that Jesus could have sent them to hell or as the scripture said, the bottomless pit, called the abyss and he said so. They were terrified of Jesus and wanted to get away intact. They did not know He would not do it at this time. As we shared earlier—they know they have a certain amount of time and that that time will come to an end, but they do not know when that will take place. They did NOT know that Jesus would not send them to the pit at this time.

The demons wanted to get away from Jesus; they could not stand to remain in His LIGHT. They wanted to go into whomever and whatever was close. Luke 8:30 (ESV), *"Jesus then asked him, 'What is your name?' And he said, 'Legion,' for many demons had entered him."* The literal translation of this is NOT 'what is your name', as if we are going to hear the personal name of the man; the request was, HOW ARE YOU CALLED or referred to, or what name do you use for yourselves, making it obvious that Jesus was addressing the demon and not the man. This was not only the deliverance of a demon from one or even two men, but the deliverance of a territory from the spirit that is over it or affects it or terrorizes it and is operating out of humanity that was housed and living in one man.

Matthew 12:43–45 ESV

> [43]"When the unclean spirit has gone out of a person, it passes through waterless places seeking rest, but finds none. [44]Then it says, 'I will return to my house from which I came.' And when it comes, it finds the house empty, swept, and put in order. [45]Then it goes and

brings with it seven other spirits more evil than itself, and they enter and dwell there, and the last state of that person is worse than the first. So also, will it be with this evil generation."

What do we know about the action of the spirit while it was away from the man? We know that it travels outside of any flesh and is seeking a place of rest. Not finding a readily available place, it goes back to where it came from hoping that it can re-enter there. Think we me for a minute about satan's temptation of Jesus in the wilderness. Luke 4:13 tells us that satan, after failing to have any effect on Jesus, came back at another time to continue his onslaught on Jesus. Luke records that the devil departed from Jesus only "for a season". The literal translation says, 'for a more suitable time'. The temptation a second time against Jesus, by satan, did not matter, because Jesus did not give into it; Jesus did not give him an inch, so, there was no reason to ever write about it or them.

In other words, even those who are demon free can expect that demons will continue to seek a haven and they look for a more suitable time when we are angry, tired or weakened by sickness or separated from loved ones, that would promise a better chance of success.

Back to the demon possessed man on the shore of the lake with Jesus. Jesus could have sent the demons into any dry area or place He chose. He could have sent them into a temple and made them remain there until their time comes—we know that today many demons occupy temples in other lands. Temples and inanimate objects are among the dry places they wander. The demons knew what Jesus could do, so they asked for the closest thing that could hold them or house them or occupy them that had life. When the pigs drowned, the demons left the bodies and went elsewhere looking for new places, not dry places and not animals, but people where they can act out their fantasies and behaviors. They wanted to be far away from Jesus and far away from His light. Evil likes darkness and cannot stand light or spiritual understanding.

Remember what we shared last time about Jesus coming to the earth incarnated as a man? John 1:1-9 says Jesus was the true light and when He came to earth verse 9 said: *He brought the light to every man that comes into the world; this is the light that gives mankind moral and spiritual insight and blocks moral darkness and evil.*

This principality had to find a new place to set up shop, because this place was no longer safe for him and his cohorts, because the Son of God was now aware of this territory;

Jesus had brought the true light the light that lights every man. The demons wanted out and away from the one person who could send them into dry places, and they knew that if Jesus said they had to remain where He sent them they must obey. The pigs ran down a step place—out of direct sight. Because of Jesus' presence they did not want to chance going back near the man they once held as a prisoner, through whom they revealed their behavior and fantasies. They were no longer, the principality over this area or territory.

Mark 3:26–27 (ESV) Jesus tells us here what happens when a believer filled with the presence of God comes around.

> [26] And if Satan has risen up against himself and is divided, he cannot stand, but is coming to an end. [27] But no one can enter a strong man's house and plunder his goods, unless he first binds the strong man. Then indeed he may plunder his house.

Jesus had come in and BOUND the strongman and the territory is now His. The demon who was in control of the man said, "Do not torment me before my time". That is a very calm and controlled way of saying what was actually said, and this is NOT how this episode took place at all. When we read this account in the NAS, it says the man bowed before Jesus, which makes it change what actually happened. That makes it wrong. The man was on his knees; he was not bowing over at the waist. The NKJV says he worshipped Him. He did NOT worship Him. What actually happened reveals that he fell to his knees in abject fear of what was coming. I have a question for us based on the original text, how does one worship, while yelling at the top of his lungs in abject fear?

Read the account with me and see that he was at the feet of Jesus cowering in fear and that is NOT worship.

Mark 5:6-8 NIV has the idea of what actually took place:

> [6]When he saw Jesus from a distance, he ran and fell on his knees in front of him. [7]He shouted at the top of his voice, "What do you want with me, Jesus, Son of the Most High God? In God's name don't torture me!" [8]For Jesus had said to him, "Come out of this man, you impure spirit!"

That is really interesting; a demon principality asking Jesus to swear to God that He will not torture him. He knew he could trust God, and not his lying boss, satan. You will notice that the demoniac was not sedate and he was not controlled, while cowering at the feet of Jesus; he was crying out in abject fear of what he thought was coming. That is not worship.

The evil spirit fell on his knees in front of the Son of God, knowing who He was, and cried out in terror, asking Jesus to swear or take an oath that He would not torture or torment him. The evil spirit knew his time would end and torment would come. In the spirit world there is no time, as we know it, and demons are not limited by space, because in the spirit, time and space is not a consideration, so, the evil spirit believed it was over for him. Evil spirits do not know when their time ENDS, but they know that it does END. If you are reading the NAS, it will lead you to believe that the evil spirit was attempting to resist Jesus—because it INCORRECTLY says in the NAS, HE HAD BEEN SAYING "COME OUT".

This is again, a strong reason why you should read several translations and one should always be the KJV. The translators for the NAS and other translations are using, meaning for meaning and not word for word; and some have taken literary license. In writing these other translations and they have misled the reader.

In regard to the boy with epilepsy that the 9 disciples could not deliver; recall that three of the 12 had been with Jesus on the mount of transfiguration. Jesus said to them 'you wicked and perverse generation', how long must I put up with your failure in faith. I have added the words failure in faith, because that is what angered Jesus.

Then Jesus asked the disciples, 'where was their faith?', I refer to the fact that they operated only through His authority and had not yet moved into faith. They were operating out of covenant and obedience and not operating in faith. The next thing is the power Jesus has over evil. The light that emanated from His spirit man could actually be recognized from a distance, by the demons.

Recall with me, when Peter in his later years walked by the sick and they were healed, it was the light that emanated from his spirit man that brought healing and that light is the Spirit of God in our inner man, our creative man. The area of our spirit man that creates or destroys. The more of him and the less of us will display a greater level of light.

Matthew 17:14-21 (KJV) Jesus is about to address the father of the boy with a demon:

¹⁴And when they were come to the multitude, there came to him a certain man, kneeling down to him, and saying,

¹⁵Lord, have mercy on my son: for he is lunatick, and sore vexed: for ofttimes he falleth into the fire, and oft into the water.

¹⁶And I brought him to thy disciples, and they could not cure him.

¹⁷Then Jesus answered and said, O faithless and perverse generation, how long shall I be with you? how long shall I suffer you? bring him hither to me.

¹⁸And Jesus rebuked the devil; and he departed out of him: and the child was cured from that very hour.

¹⁹Then came the disciples to Jesus apart, and said, Why could not we cast him out?

²⁰And Jesus said unto them, Because of your unbelief: for verily I say unto you, If ye have faith as a grain of mustard seed, ye shall say

> unto this mountain, Remove hence to yonder place; and it shall remove; and nothing shall be impossible unto you.
>
> ²¹Howbeit [or however] this kind goeth not out but by prayer and fasting.

Again, in verse 21 we see a higher level of power and influence/or authority. The disciples tried to cast out the devil, but could not.

When Jesus came, the demon felt compelled to leave and left so violently he tore at the boy and left him on the ground. Please notice the demon felt compelled to leave before Jesus ever spoke a word.

Jesus said, just prior to this incident, and he is referring to all believers and not just Peter, "where is your faith?" Once again, if you are reading an NIV, NAS, TLB or an RSV, then your bible does not have verse 21; in fact, it goes from 20 to verse 22. The theme of the passage, as it climaxes in verse 20, is that a small amount of faith could move mountains—even a mustard seed amount. **How could demons stand against this tiny bit of true faith?**

The disciples are being taken to task for not having even that much faith. We do not in general understand the idea of a mustard seed amount of faith. And many of us are just now learning what faith actually is, not what we have thought or been taught all these centuries that is wrong. It is not about the size of the seed, but instead it is the fact that even the smallest amount of real faith can move the mountains in our lives. The same holds true with the mustard seed amount of faith. The mustard seed is supposed to grow. This section in 13:31 of Matthew is about growing the seed of faith. The important thing to remember about the seed is its beginning size is a reference to potential, and NOT its ARRIVAL.

The idea behind the size of the seed is that from that little faith can come great things. The tiny seed has the ability to become a towering plant or even a tree. Even a little faith in the divine promises of God, will at the right moment, become a mighty power and accomplish wonders.

There were 9 disciples who failed to bring deliverance to that epileptic boy. The miracle was not dependent on the boy or his father, or even the multitude; it was dependent on the 9 disciples, who showed they did not have the mustard seed size of faith for this miracle, yet they were doing other great miracles. Matthew is referring back to chapter 13:31-32 (KJV) because he has already used it.

> ³¹Another parable put he forth unto them, saying, The kingdom of heaven is like to a grain of mustard seed, which a man took, and sowed in his field:
>
> ³²Which indeed is the least of all seeds: but when it is grown, it is the greatest among herbs, and becometh a tree, so that the birds of the air come and lodge in the branches thereof.

The mustard seed is an illustration of NOT what is, but what could be, when the seed is planted in good soil. Even the text tells us, when it is sown it is very small, but then it says, when it is grown, look how big it can become. From Proverbs 20: 27 we see that we are the soil that has been prepared to receive the seed, and from this planting, God is expecting that out of us will grow a great tree that becomes a place of rest and protection for those whose lives we influence. We are the soil, and Jesus is the seed who has been planted in us by God

Proverbs 20:27 (KJV), *"The spirit of man is the candle of the LORD, searching all the inward parts of the belly."* The word for candle that He uses does NOT mean lamp or light or candle, as we understand the word today. The word He used means the gleam or the light that shines, because of the oil of anointing. Its equal meaning refers to tilling the soil. It is the light God sees in man and it creates the glistening or gleam in God's eye, when He sees the flame that He has soaked with His Spirit, beginning to come alive in His child.

Colossians 2:8–10 HCSB

> [8]Be careful that no one takes you captive through philosophy and empty deceit based on human tradition, based on the elemental forces of the world, and not based on Christ. [9]For the entire fullness of God's nature dwells bodily in Christ, [10]and you have been filled by Him, who is the head over every ruler and authority.

So, who does God see, when He sees me? Jesus said, **I am as He is** (see 1 John 4:17). He sees a fresh furrow, where His planted seed, and that seed is Jesus in me, growing into a tree, "whose leaf will not wither [and] whatsoever this tree does will prosper" (Psalm 1:3 HCSB) and when this tree is grown, it will provide shade and warmth and protection to those who want to be under its branches.

The redeemed spirit of man is the gleam in God's eye, as He is searching all the inward parts of our emotional hunger in the spirit and the basis of our understanding that He has placed in our spirit man. This is a direct reference to the effort we are putting forth to become all that He said we could be in Him and that includes our taking the dominion Jesus has given us over this earth where we have been destined to rule as His under gods.

Matthew 13:31-32 (KJV) Jesus is teaching the multitude and using parables:

> [31]Another parable put he forth unto them, saying, The kingdom of heaven is like to a grain of mustard seed, which a man took, and sowed in his field:
>
> [32]Which indeed is the least of all seeds: but when it is grown, it is the greatest among herbs, and becometh a tree, so that the birds of the air come and lodge in the branches thereof.

The mustard seed is an illustration of NOT what is, but what could be, when the seed is planted in good soil. Even the text tells us, when it is sown it is very small, but then it says, when it is grown, look how big it can become.

My question to me, and now to you is, What am I doing to grow my seed that God has planted in me to cause me to become all that He said I was to be?

CHAPTER FIVE

From Proverbs 20: 27 we see that we are the soil that has been prepared to receive the seed, and from this planting, God is expecting that out of us will grow a great tree. A tree that becomes a place of rest and protection for those, whose lives we influence.

Proverbs 20:27 ESV

> [27]The spirit of man is the lamp of the LORD,
> searching all his innermost parts.

The word for lamp that He uses does NOT mean lamp or light or candle, as we understand the word today. The word He uses means the gleam or the light that shines, because of the oil of anointing. Its equal meaning refers to tilling the soil. It is the glistening or gleam in God's eye, when He sees the flame that He has soaked with His Spirit, beginning to come alive in His child. Why is He searching the innermost parts, the belly? Because this is where God has located the soil of our creative nature. This is where He has located the soil of our redeemed spirit man, which has been tilled, and where HE sees the gleam of a fresh furrow.

This picture in the spirit means this man is ready for God's seed to grow. We are the field and God is the man in this parable who has planted the seed. When He planted it, it was the least of all seeds; it began as an IDEA, but when it is grown it is greater than all herbs and becomes a tree. God's seed placed in the man or woman who is ready, and has a heart that is prepared, becomes so visible that God sees a fresh furrow that is ready for Him to plant, to place the seed of the potential of God; which is planting or establishing this man or woman, and watch them become a tree and stand with dominion in the kingdom of God, which Jesus said, "has come to earth".

God's seed is His word, and His word is Jesus, and God sent His word, Jesus, to the earth, incarnated as a man, to be God's planting in the earth, to restore what the devil received from Adam and Eve when they sinned and broke trust with God. When we are in fellowship with God, and break trust and go back to where we were before, before we invited Him into our lives, we have not only lost valuable ground, but time and potential that has to be recovered, and with God it can happen overnight and we can get back on track, but please know that even when we get back on track the devil has total recall and he will use all of our past foolishness to cause us to surrender again to his temptations. he knows how and when to push our buttons.

Jesus was sent to the earth to be planted in God's creation, mankind, and restore all that was lost, and given by Adam and Eve to satan, and when mankind sees who God is in himself or herself, they become the furrow in the soil and God sees them, and plants them in the earth to become His trees.

Psalm 1:1–3 KJV

> [1]Blessed is the man That walketh not in the counsel of the ungodly, Nor standeth in the way of sinners, Nor sitteth in the seat of the scornful.
>
> [2]But his delight is in the law of the LORD; And in his law doth he meditate day and night.
>
> [3]And he shall be like a tree planted by the rivers of water, That bringeth forth his fruit in his season; His leaf also shall not wither; And whatsoever he doeth shall prosper.

Rivers of water can, and often do refer to Holy Spirit, and here in this verse, we become planted by Holy Spirit and we start to produce the fruit that we were created to bear. Verse 3 tells us this person's leaf will not wither, which means whatever sprouts from this person will not fall away in disgrace or fail to become something. Whatever this person, who is now seen as a tree does, will accomplish and fulfil its intended purpose, and that purpose will be profitable and this tree will become what they have set out to accomplish. Now we have become the planting and we bear the fruit, and what we do becomes permanent and it prospers in the kingdom of God that has come to the earth.

When the word says planted by the rivers of water in this sentence, it is actually more accurate to say, taken from where it was to someplace else, by the spirit and transplanted by the rivers of water. And the rivers of water in this verse refer to Holy Spirit and His placement of this tree; this person who has become the fruit of the seed of Christ.

This is a direct statement that relates to being transplanted by Holy Spirit taking us from being planted where we were, to a position of His choice; within His calling and God's written plan for us, planned before the foundation of the earth and printed in a book in heaven and catalogued under our name with the results of our lives as we live upon this earth.

We have taken that too lightly, too casually as if to say, that sounds good, BUT. We must reconsider the magnitude of what we just heard. The God of the universe has written a plan about me and a plan about you and it has been written even before the foundation of the earth. How important then is this plan about me? This is really a powerful thing that has now happened to the redeemed person who is sold out to the Lord and committed to walk as Jesus walked, but how did we get here. Please let me remind the body of Christ about two separate parables where the Lord of the manor or the Lord of the land went on a far trip and left his servants in charge [servants are those who are committed to the Lord or master] and gave each of them money to do whatever was necessary during his absence. No one has to agree with what I am writing, but do yourself a favor... At the very least, consider what you are about to read concerning the Lord of the kingdom and His servants and how He may look at our inactivity in His kingdom, now that He has blessed us with favor.

When the Lord comes back from his trip in each of these scenarios, he brings his servants in and has each one of them give an account of what they did with the money he left them. In the account in Matthew's gospel, one servant is given one talent, another is given two, and to the third 5 talents; in Luke's account the Lord gives each of the servants one talent and asks them also to give Him an account of what they did with the money. The point of these two different accounts is usually missed by the reader and is the reason for the parable. To each one of us are given gifts or talents and these talents and or gifts are for us to use in the kingdom of God here on the earth, and they are based upon our natural gifts and intelligence, which have also been given to us by God. Often after we have been walking as a believer for some period of time many men and women sit down at home with all this talent and all these spiritual gifts doing nothing, and nothing is Unacceptable to God and He has said this, using the parable of the talents using gifts from a small amount to a large amount to reveal what He thinks about body members being inactive and unproductive.

The end result is simply this; most of the body of Christ is sitting home and has not been using the spiritual gifts or talents for the Lord either, because it is inconvenient or they think they have done what was necessary and someone else needs to take the helm and that is a lie from the devil.

On the day of accounting the Lord God Almighty will be seated on His throne and He will ask each of us what did we do with Jesus and what did we do with our gifts and talents, and WHO ON EARTH TOLD US WE COULD SIT DOWN AND PASS THE BUCK or DUTY, TO SOMEONE ELSE????

Luke 19:12–13 KJV

> [12] Jesus said therefore, A certain nobleman went into a far country to receive for himself a kingdom, and to return.
>
> [13] And he called his ten servants, and delivered them ten pounds, and said unto them, Occupy till I come.

The word *OCCUPY* means to engage in the business at hand and keep it moving. When we read this story, we see that not all of them did what they were told to do. Do not forget there were ten of them in this account and ten in the bible is the number of completeness, not 7. The use of the number 10 reveals that each person, every one of us is given gifts and talents based upon our genetic and spiritual makeup and our use of these is judged by God, based upon our potential in His eyes, and that makes it fair to all mankind, revealing again that God is no respecter of any person over another. 7 is the number of completed dealings in the rule of mankind by heaven, not the number of completeness.

Luke 19:15–17 HCSB

> [15] "At his return, having received the authority to be king, he summoned those slaves he had

given the money to, so he could find out how much they had made in business. ¹⁶The first came forward and said, 'Master, your mina has earned 10 more minas.'

¹⁷"'Well done, good slave!' he told him. 'Because you have been faithful in a very small matter, have authority over 10 towns.'"

Another gave his account and increased what he was given and then another who did not do as he was expected to do came in and gave his excuse why. There were ten in total, only as a representation that each person born into this world has the same opportunity in the eyes of God. Look at what the reward was; he was given to rule over towns and people. The reward is not based upon money, the reward is based upon using the gifts and talents; the reward was based upon obedience to continue the work that was before them. Consider with me that the gift or reward was authority over people and towns. These men became shepherds, which is the greatest occupation under God that anyone can be given, because it reveals how much trust God has in us.

Luke 19:20–22 HCSB

> [20]"And another came and said, 'Master, here is your mina. I have kept it hidden away in a cloth [21]because I was afraid of you, for you're a tough man: you collect what you didn't deposit and reap what you didn't sow.'
>
> [22]"He told him, 'I will judge you by what you have said, you evil slave! If you knew I was a tough man, collecting what I didn't deposit and reaping what I didn't sow.'"

This man went in front of his Lord, as if he had a cause or a reason to do nothing, knowing the Lord would judge his actions. His behavior was based upon his fear and his fear kept him from performing the duties and requirements that all of us have been given, based upon our God given abilities. Then the Lord told those servants who were standing with this one to take away the money and give it to the one who had increased his by the greatest amount.

Luke 19:26–27 HCSB

> [26]"'I tell you, that to everyone who has, more will be given; and from the one who does not have, even what he does have will be taken

away. ²⁷But bring here these enemies of mine,
who did not want me to rule over them, and
slaughter them in my presence.'"

I have never heard anyone of these accounts shared as we shared them here, but believe me, that is what I believe will happen to the body of believers who are doing nothing and yet have been given gifts and talents to build the kingdom.

Go back with me to a previous chapter and see that Jesus was speaking to men He had chosen, who made a purposeful decision to give their lives over to Him and read with me the backup of how those who have committed and become all they can be in the Lord, have been given all that is necessary to fulfill the plan and purpose that God has written about them. And if God did that for them, He has done that for us, because time and the date on the wall do not have any effect on God's word, when He said that He is no respecter of one person over the other.

This conversation began with Matthew 16:1–2 (HCSB):

¹The Pharisees and Sadducees approached, and
as a test, asked Him to show them a sign from
heaven.

²He answered them: "When evening comes you say, 'It will be good weather because the sky is red.'

Jesus has discussed with them the weather and the signs that reveal what weather is coming. Jesus then said to them, that they were an evil generation who came seeking a sign. So, unless this group changes the way it thinks, they are no longer given any consideration, as those who are yet to come.

Matthew 16:5–12 ESV

⁵When the disciples reached the other side, they had forgotten to bring any bread. ⁶Jesus said to them, "Watch and beware of the leaven of the Pharisees and Sadducees." ⁷And they began discussing it among themselves, saying, "We brought no bread." ⁸But Jesus, aware of this, said, "O you of little faith, why are you discussing among yourselves the fact that you have no bread? ⁹Do you not yet perceive? Do you not remember the five loaves for the five thousand, and how many baskets you gathered? ¹⁰Or the seven loaves for the four thousand, and how many baskets you gathered? ¹¹How is it that

you fail to understand that I did not speak about bread? Beware of the leaven of the Pharisees and Sadducees." [12]Then they understood that he did not tell them to beware of the leaven of bread, but of the teaching of the Pharisees and Sadducees.

So, leaven is false teaching that has been added to the truth. And in this case the false teaching has been added by the leadership. Jesus has chosen fishermen who are not world wise, and who lack formal education and is walking with them to create disciples who spiritually understand the world and all that can and does impact mankind. Stop and consider what Jesus is doing with mere men.

These are men who are somewhat ignorant and unlearned, but intelligent, willing and able to hear wisdom, and learn from someone who has all that they will ever need; Matthew of course was quite different, and was educated in numbers. This is a sample for all the rest of us in the world, who would hear about Jesus and decide to follow Him and adhere to what He says or walk away from Him and say I am not interested, I choose the world instead. Just like the men we just read about, the Pharisees and the Sadducees.

Matthew 16:13–20 ESV (commentary added)

[13]Now when Jesus came into the district of Caesarea Philippi, he asked his disciples, "Who do people say that the Son of Man is?" [14]And they said, "Some say John the Baptist, others say Elijah, and others Jeremiah or one of the prophets." [15]He said to them, "But who do you say that I am?" [16]Simon Peter replied, "You are the Christ, the Son of the living God." [17]And Jesus answered him, "Blessed are you, Simon Bar-Jonah! For flesh and blood has not revealed this to you, but my Father who is in heaven. [18]And I tell you, you are Peter, and on this rock, I will build my church, and the gates of hell shall not prevail against it.

[verse 16 is the rock Jesus is speaking about; referring to the knowledge that Jesus is the Christ, the Son of God]

[19]I will give you the keys of the kingdom of heaven, and whatever you bind on earth shall be bound in heaven, and whatever you loose on earth shall be loosed in heaven." [20]Then he

strictly charged the disciples to tell no one that
he was the Christ.

The church needs to pick up the keys. These keys are for His kingdom here on the earth. We all know that we do not need keys in heaven. There were 12 original apostles; one of them we know is in hell; yet he was offered the keys and refused them and he was among those who were casting out demons and healing the sick.

Have you thought that the same spirit that kept Judas from taking the keys is alive and well and leading some denominations and religions? I mean no offense, but isn't it time to wake up and see what they have done to the church and by that, I mean the real church, not the club churches, but the church as Jesus sees the church? The one the 1st century church could actually recognize, because it looks just like they did in spirit and truth. Keys, we know represent authority and denote power and ownership. *"Will I keep my own words to my own hurt, so that my honor cannot be questioned, or do I waver, because the battle I am in gets too hot?"* Is it my way, instead of His way, and do I worship God with all the other things that one might think I worship, because of how they have become my first priority? What's in your belly, your innermost being? What is in any of us? How does God see me and who does He see when He sees me? Who are we really in the body of Christ? and when we say, "such as I have I give unto you," do we know what we have — what do we really have and what are we made of?

Many groups have replaced authority and power with works and traditions and programs that have reduced the believer to living without power, and because of that, they are walking around trying to make it, and never seeming to make it beyond the most basic level of relationship with Jesus. Many remain carnal, their speech is worldly and their faith it based upon, 'IF IT BE THY WILL'. And because they do not know the word of God for themselves, they do not know God's will, so many of their prayers appear to be based on nothing more than HOPE or NEED or DESIRE or LONGING, and even CHANCE and they give no appearance of a relationship with Jesus. They are not distinguishable from the lost souls of the world, except on occasion in their conversations. They carry no keys; Holy Spirit is not allowed to function in them — they have been taught HE was for the 1st century church ONLY. They have been taught that those of us who believe in His active participation in our lives are deranged or challenged or overzealous.

Keys are given only to those who can be trusted with them and that does not include everyone who joins the club, it includes those members who have learned the rules and operate within them and have been proven over time that they can be trusted with the keys. Everyone does not get the keys, because not everyone is trustworthy. No matter how many times they quote the scripture that says we have been given the keys. Quoting scripture about keys is NOT possession or authority or ownership. Why were Peter and by association the 12 apostles offered the keys?

Matthew 16:18-19 ESV

> [18]And I tell you, you are Peter, and on this rock I will build my church, and the gates of hell shall not prevail against it. [19]I will give you the keys of the kingdom of heaven, and whatever you bind on earth shall be bound in heaven, and whatever you loose on earth shall be loosed[c] in heaven."

Peter, and by association the apostles, were offered the keys because they NOW knew by association and behavior, who Jesus was, and they had become a part of all that He was doing. They were all in. The keys came, because they were committed and knew what was required. The kingdom of heaven that has come to earth is not about words without power. The church is NEVER to be full of words and empty of power, like it has become. It is way past time for the church to become involved, and in love with its Lord.

Paul the apostle is very aware that there is a lot of talking going on in the church and that most of it is being done by those who reveal they have very little or NO power.

1 Corinthians 4:19–20 (ESV) Paul tells the church at Corinth:

> [19]But I will come to you soon, if the Lord wills, and I will find out not the talk of these arrogant people but their power. [20]For the kingdom of God does not consist in talk but in power.

I do not wish to speak for or about others, because we, you and I are in jeopardy of being the same way; speaking many words without power and being no different than the world we have become free of. It is time to put away the foolishness that we have made important and find out who we are in Christ, and become that person who thinks and acts and operates in that power; the power of God given to mankind to take dominion over the earth and everything that is in the earth, including our own selves. It is time to make the God we say we love and serve, the priority in our lives.

It is time to get real with ourselves and real with God. Americans have made everything else the priority and God has become just another tag-along, exactly like Israel did, just before God sent judgment upon them.

In no time at all, Peter, as many have done, went from receiving the keys to the kingdom to being on the outside looking in...to what he let go of.

Matthew 16:23 ESV

> [23]But Jesus turned and said to Peter, "Get behind me, Satan! You are a hindrance to me. For you are not setting your mind on the things of God, but on the things of man."

Just because something is offered, does not mean that it is accepted. Peter's old man speaks out and Jesus rebukes him, "get thee behind me satan, thou art an offense to me." That is all we hear of that verse, but the remainder is where the emphasis is placed.

Jesus is continuing to teach His disciples and in verse 24.

Matthew 16:24–25 ESV

> [24] Then Jesus told his disciples, "If anyone would come after me, let him deny himself and take up his cross and follow me. [25] For whoever would save his life will lose it, but whoever loses his life for my sake will find it.

Have you ever really thought about what He just said? *If you lose your life you will find it.* Think with me about that; He is NOT talking about death, because at this stage of the conversation that would be pointless and worthless. When we decide to lose our life in His life, we have found the real life and the actual life and the future God has always planned for us. As Jeremiah said in 29:11, God has written plans for us that include only the good things of this kingdom and there is no loss to us in these plans, there is no harm intended to bring us to this place of success in Christ.

The cross that we take up is the decision, daily, to let Jesus be lord instead of us. It is easy to say this or write this out on a piece of paper, but much harder to walk it out in the days and the weeks ahead. Each day that we set out to walk with God, is a day that the enemy is being challenged, and since we created the challenge we need to be sharp and ready as well as responsive, when the enemy sends whatever he has decided to send at us that day.

Peter was displaying the self-attitude and not, the let Jesus be lord attitude. We want to be our own lord—what makes me say that? We want to take offense when it is unnecessary and we want to hold onto to it when it is actually smarter to let it go. We want to do things our way, because we think our plan should be His plan—for instance, when we are doing nothing of consequence and get a gentle nudge by the Spirit that comes into our mind telling us to leave the TV or some other thing we are doing and go pray—we tell ourselves it will be more convenient later. We do not want to deny our natural desire in favor of His desire, and because of that we cannot walk as HE would have walked, if He was still here as a man, by behaving that way.

Luke 22:31–33 (ESV) Jesus is addressing Simon Peter:

> [31]"Simon, Simon, behold, Satan demanded to have you, that he might sift you like wheat, [32]but I have prayed for you that your faith may not fail."

If Jesus was operating as God at this time, He would have no need to pray—but He prayed, because he was functioning or operating as a man.

[31b]"And when you have turned again, strengthen your brothers."

[33]Peter said to him, "Lord, I am ready to go with you both to prison and to death."

Peter meant what he said—but we all know that he failed, and did not do what he said he would do. His words ended up powerless, they came out of his soul, his mind, will and emotion, which was full of self, so, his words were empty. Until Peter surrendered his self-will for God's will, he would remain empty and powerless. The same holds true for us as well.

Jesus told Peter, "when you are converted", which means change the direction of your life. He was told this, after 3 years of walking and listening to Jesus every day. Jesus said, "Peter when you let Me be Lord, instead of you, help your brothers." Peter when you have true trust and confidence in Me, and that can only come, after you change the direction of your life, help your brothers turn with resolve in the same direction. Peter was lacking in faith, and so were the disciples.

Peter's lack of self-denial, and his failure to control his flesh was what Jesus was addressing. It takes faith to let go, and without faith you cannot let go, and that is what we call fear. The disciples were prepared to walk in COVENANT, but they had to learn to walk in faith and operate in faith and we must learn that as well. Peter was full of pride, which gave the devil place. Ephesians 4:27 tells us to give the devil NO place. Among the disciples, who were called Apostles, who was the oldest, and the boldest, and who walked on water? Peter. However, All the disciples had the same problem, pride.

Mark 9:17–24 NKJV

> [17]Then one of the crowd answered and said, "Teacher, I brought You my son, who has a mute spirit. [18]And wherever it seizes him, it throws him down; he foams at the mouth, gnashes his teeth, and becomes rigid. So, I spoke to Your disciples, that they should cast it out, but they could not."
>
> [19]He answered him and said, "O faithless generation, how long shall I be with you? How long shall I bear with you? Bring him to Me." [20]Then they brought him to Him. And when he saw Him, immediately the spirit convulsed him, and he fell on the ground and wallowed, foaming at the mouth.

²¹So He asked his father, "How long has this been happening to him?"

And he said, "From childhood. ²²And often he has thrown him both into the fire and into the water to destroy him. But if You can do anything, have compassion on us and help us."

²³Jesus said to him, "If you can believe, all things are possible to him who believes."

²⁴Immediately the father of the child cried out and said with tears, "Lord, I believe; help my unbelief!"

From that point until this, too many have used what this man said when their faith was not sufficient, and sadly it was never meant as a panacea for the faithless. We need to spend time with the Father, so that we move out or away from unbelief. This man did not have that relation with Father God or knowledge; he was doing the best he could do. Do not forget that 9 of the Apostles of Jesus already failed

In the next series of verses, that we will read together, there are three keys to unlocking what was going on with the disciples. **Listen carefully, so that you can hear them.**

Mark 9:25–34 (NKJV)

> [25]When Jesus saw that the people came running together, He rebuked the unclean spirit, saying to it, "Deaf and dumb spirit, I command you, come out of him and enter him no more!" [26]Then the spirit cried out, convulsed him greatly, and came out of him. And he became as one dead, so that many said, "He is dead." [27]But Jesus took him by the hand and lifted him up, and he arose.
>
> [28]And when He had come into the house, His disciples asked Him privately, "Why could we not cast it out?"

[29]So He said to them, "This kind can come out by nothing but prayer and fasting."

> [30]Then they departed from there and passed through Galilee, and He did not want anyone to know it. [31]For He taught His disciples and said to them, "The Son of Man is being betrayed into the hands of men, and they will kill Him. And after He is killed, He will rise the third day."

> [32] But they did not understand this saying, and were afraid to ask Him.
>
> [33] Then He came to Capernaum. And when He was in the house He asked them, "What was it you disputed among yourselves on the road?" [34] But they kept silent, for on the road they had disputed among themselves who would be the greatest.

Earlier we read Matthew 17 and Matthew's view, and now we see the view that Mark takes in his account of this part of the works of Jesus. Please notice that the disciples could not cast out the demon from the boy and after Jesus told them why, they asked which one of us will be the greatest? They were not passionate about the work of Christ; they were interested in position. Jesus told them that fasting and prayer was required to change their thinking and attitudes. The flesh had a hold on them and not the spirit. Their deeds had been done, because of Jesus and now the time had come for them to take control of their own flesh. This is best done by fasting, because fasting with prayer humbles the flesh, and earnest prayer, opens communication with the Father. Fasting without prayer is called dieting.

In the early stages of the disciples walk in this new power, the demons and the spirit world were confused, but now they had re-positioned themselves and saw that without Jesus the disciples were walking in the flesh and flesh cannot cast out flesh or demons. They were still operating in the flesh and not denying self; they were still operating in unbelief. They did not have true compassion, because they lacked passion for the people and in their minds and hearts the issue was, "who will be 1st, and if I am not first, then what position will I have?"

Matthew 18:1–3 (NKJV)

> [1]At that time the disciples came to Jesus, saying, "Who then is greatest in the kingdom of heaven?"
>
> [2]Then Jesus called a little child to Him, set him in the midst of them, [3]and said, "Assuredly, I say to you, unless you are converted and become as little children, you will by no means enter the kingdom of heaven."

Except or on the condition that you be converted [that means change your thinking and your behavior] and become as little children, whose motives are pure, and whose lives are innocent and without personal agendas, you will not enter the kingdom of heaven. Please notice that little children do not carry OFFENSES with them and they do not understand even a little bit, what revenge is or why it is done. Jesus was talking about His kingdom here on earth. He was talking about the kingdom He brought here to establish it on the earth. They had already accepted that Jesus was the Christ—the son of the living God, so they were assured of Heaven—but that is not what Jesus was speaking about.

He was telling them that here on planet earth is a place where the disciples of Jesus could enter, and live way above those on planet earth, who have not changed their worldly thinking into Christ-like thinking. They could live by the same principles that Jesus did and with the same successes. Catch that. Jesus is telling his disciples, AFTER 3 YEARS OF WALKING DAILY WITH HIM, to get converted, change their ways; become like Him and later we see they did. Later they became men of fasting and prayer with only the gospel as their agenda. To the extent, they willingly offered their lives to the good news of Jesus. They had already performed the miracles; but when the devil realized he could stand against them and win, he stood. He was caught off guard by the disciples initially, because of the presence of Jesus.

Later when he stood his ground in Matthew 17 they could not withstand him, because they lacked faith, they lacked assurance; they had SELF in the way. They in and of themselves did not know who they were; he sensed it, stood against them and prevailed. The disciples lacked assurance.

Recall Abraham and Sarah had been given assurance by God—that assurance being the title deed. That assurance, that faith, that substance or foundation did a re-creative miracle. It brought back to life—two sexually dead bodies. Jesus, on the other hand, lacked nothing and when he left us, he said "it is yours to do now, but wait until Holy Spirit empowers you." Before you move out from here to do anything". Do not go anywhere UNTIL He comes upon you, and they did what He said to do, but understand this—He only comes upon those who are asking and waiting for Him—not upon those who reject Him or do not believe He is here now.

Allow me to discuss the word ASSURANCE for clarity. In the Greek, the word for substance is *HUPOSTASIS* or assurance. It is the title deed or legal paper to faith.

Hebrews 11:1 NKJV

> ¹Now faith is the substance of things hoped for,
> the evidence of things not seen.

Substance is the legal paper to faith—the title deed. [5287 hupostasis]-Substance is the thing that is put under; it is a substructure, or becomes a foundation; it is designed to keep that which is above it stable.

Your faith in Jesus is the substance or foundation of your salvation. It creates 7 things: it has *actual existence*; it has *substance*, it is *real*. It has become steadfastness in your mind, a firmness of your position, a raw courage, a committed resolution, relentless confidence, a firm trust, the assurance. *HUPO* stasis comes from the base word *HUPO* meaning UNDER and *STASIS* comes from the base word *HISTEMI*, which means to stand your ground or watch what was appointed to you or hold fast to the covenant. Our medical word for antihistamines comes from this word; an antihistamine is a medicine that stands against something.

Be resolute because you have firm trust in your belly; and your belly is the womb of the place of creation that comes from you. It is the place where we all create from our faith or destroy from our doubt and fear. And forget your schedule; God is not working on your time schedule, so He is not required to live up to your schedule. We are told to wait on the Lord, but in a fast-food world, we are affected by the general attitude around us, even our prayer life is fast food driven.

Once you have the substance, the legal title, whether you see it or not legally those things are bound to come to you, because legally they now belong to you. This is about the law. It may not happen today or tomorrow, but if you have been given the assurance, the substance, the Rhema word from God while in your prayer closet, then you will get what you have requested.

What's in your belly. What is in any of us? Who are we really in the body of Christ? and when we see someone in need do we have what Peter had when he said, "such as I have I give unto you," do we even know what we have—what do we really have and what are we made of?

<u>Now</u> is the time to learn who we are—now is the time to tell others to come to Christ.

<u>Now</u> is the time to lay hands on the sick in our circle of influence and expect God to intervene.

<u>Now</u> is the time to check our relationship with Jesus, and as Paul the apostle told us; examine yourselves and see what and who is really in you.

<u>Now</u> is the time to exercise our spiritual gifts, so that we know when we say, "such as I haven I give unto you", we know what we have by use and by personal experience.

CHAPTER SIX

Often people who are seeking God or seeking a better life, have questions that either are not answered or are not answered completely or sufficiently. One of those questions is, "Why do I go through what I go through, if God loves me so much"? Because after you repent and turn away from sin, God sees you as a son, and because He sees you as a son, He disciplines you as His son. Now who does God see when He sees me? Male or female He sees you as a son.

Please let me start with the person God loved more than any other person and use Him as the example that answers that question, and that person is Jesus. God chastened Jesus and He never sinned, because the Lord chastens those He loves, and He said so. And He does it to make us become better and greater, and separate us from the crowd.

Proverbs 3:11-12 HCSB (commentary added)

> [11]Do not despise the LORD's instruction, my son,
> and do not loathe His discipline;

¹²for the LORD disciplines the one He loves,
just as a father, the son he delights in.

[corrects, rebukes, proves; and proves is a picture word showing a father arguing with His sons, which causes them to see the truth over what they were thinking that was wrong]

Hebrews 12:4-8 HCSB (insertion added)

⁴In struggling against sin, you have not yet resisted to the point of shedding your blood. ⁵And you have forgotten the exhortation that addresses you as sons:

My son, do not take the Lord's discipline lightly
or faint when you are reproved by Him,
⁶for the Lord disciplines the one He loves
and punishes every son He receives.

⁷Endure *[suffering]* as discipline: God is dealing with you as sons. For what son is there that a father does not discipline? ⁸But if you are without discipline—which all receive—then you are illegitimate children and not sons.

We have asked questions that mislead us, when we ask, why do I go through what I do? because we have grown up thinking it is all about me—and it is not all about me, however, I am included in what it is about.

God hears us, but often the request will take time to answer, because God is working in us to perfect us, and He is not some Santa clause that jumps up, because we have just come to understand that He is real, and our life feels like a quagmire, sucking us farther down each day. We are being refined and challenged and seasoned, because God loves us as sons. And correct discipline from a loving father guides us to greatness. We want God to speak to us this minute, right now, and the very next minute we are off to do what we want or worse, what we should not do, all the time expecting God to speak to us. We never stop and think about how we can get His attention and give Him a reason to speak to us—because, again, we think it is all about us to the exclusion of others, as well as God. From the time we were little, when we cried; we got attention. That's over.

There must be a real desire to change and until then, there is not a focus on us any more than the liar and the thief and the murderer, because we maintain the thinking that it is all about us, what we want to do, to the exclusion of others.

God changes our world when we choose to enter His world, the world He made for us. When we seek Him, really go after Him, and decide to turn away from who we have become, and who we are now, because we have seen enough of who we are now, to want that changed or stopped or recreated, and we want another person, a changed us, living in our body; then God will help us change our life.

Jeremiah 29:13 (HCSB) God tells Jeremiah:

> [13]You will seek Me and find Me when you search for Me with all your heart.

Now we have an answer to our question, and now we are on the radar. When we want the person, we have been for way too long, to be the person God wants us to be; when we come to the end of ourselves, and realize we are making a mess of our lives without God, or at the very least we are not accomplishing our goals, it is then we find God. For some, the goals have become covered over with sadness and depression and the feeling of what is the use—it is always same old thing, do this, do that, same old thing, just a different day.

When we seek God with all of our heart, we have been promised that we will find Him, but in truth, He will find us—

we need to find Him, not just the words on a page about Him, but Him. He is the one who is jealous for us—read it with me.

Exodus 20:4-5 HCSB

> ⁴Do not make an idol for yourself, whether in the shape of anything in the heavens above or on the earth below or in the waters under the earth. ⁵You must not bow down to them or worship them; for I, the LORD your God, am a jealous God, punishing the children for the fathers' sin, to the third and fourth generations of those who hate Me.

We often think an idol is just a figure or a statue that people worship, but that is not what the word means here. An idol can be anything we place more time, effort, or thinking about than our relationship with Him. It can be our enthusiasm for sports or our job or our money or car, boat, house, person or even our leisure activities—our free time.

Where does our money, time and effort go, when we are able to make the choice of where we use them? That is who or what our idol is, and very often that has come ahead of God.

Malachi 3:7–10 NIV

> ⁷Ever since the time of your ancestors you have turned away from my decrees and have not kept them. Return to me, and I will return to you," says the LORD Almighty.
>
> "But you ask, 'How are we to return?'
>
> ⁸"Will a mere mortal rob God? Yet you rob me.
>
> "But you ask, 'How are we robbing you?'
>
> "In tithes and offerings. ⁹You are under a curse—your whole nation—because you are robbing me. ¹⁰Bring the whole tithe into the storehouse, that there may be food in my house. Test me in this," says the LORD Almighty, "and see if I will not throw open the floodgates of heaven and pour out so much blessing that there will not be room enough to store it."

If you are using your tithing money, then you are the ones God is speaking to and about. God has used this pandemic that recently shut down the world, to give the world a chance to get off the merry-go-round, and find once again what is important and eternal, because not one of the things I have mentioned can establish our place in eternity. And yet too many of us act like they are, and because of our treatment of these other things, they have become idols—idols that take away our time, money, focus, potential, and even our eternity with the God who made us. Some say they are uncomfortable with that, but God says, it is not about your comfort, it is about your eternity. It is about our walk with God, and our relationship with Him.

It is about the journey we are on and the experiences of our lives as we take this journey with Him. God wants to walk with us, talk with us and guide us, but since time began, too many people and too many in churches have merely told us don't do this or that or eat this or that, and don't drink this or that, and make sure you wear your clothes a certain way or blah blah blah, and NOT ONE of those things has any place in our eternity—It is what we choose to do that matters for our eternity. It is the choices we make that determine our eternity.

Matthew 15:11 HCSB

> [11]"It's not what goes into the mouth that defiles a man, but what comes out of the mouth, this defiles a man."

Mark 7:15 HCSB

> [15] "Nothing that goes into a person from outside can defile him, but the things that come out of a person are what defile him."

God wants a relationship with us, but instead of being taught how to obtain that relationship, and walk and talk with Him, we have been given a set of man-made rules, rules that for the most part we will break. It is obvious the church has not learned yet from Israel's mistakes; God chose Israel above all groups and gave them grace to learn and walk with Him, but they surrendered God's grace for rules, and then repeatedly broke every one of them. We are not capable of keeping the laws that God has implemented without His help. People gravitate to using rules, because they have failed to have a relationship with the law giver.

Without a relationship with someone we cannot know what a person is thinking. It is the relationship that causes us to keep the rules, because we do not want to break that fellowship by doing something stupid, and we do not have to be told what is stupid or sinful, we know instinctively, and Romans confirms that. It is His Spirit that moves us away from evil and toward good—not rules. It is a marriage with a physical, emotional and spiritual relationship and not an affair we have on Sunday, while the rest of the week we are busy with our relationship with the world and our habits and hobbies and our idols.

Another question the world keeps throwing at the church is "why is the church full of HYPOCRITES". How many times have we heard people tells us, "we don't go to church, because it is full of hypocrites". I have TWO answers for that;

1. What better place could they be?
2. What does any hypocrite have to do with what we do, or what we are required to do, or choose to do?

Will we be standing with them at the judgment seat of God, because of that? Why call someone ELSE a hypocrite when the person using that word knows enough about God to be called by that name as well? That is a very poor excuse for us to deny what we are required to do.

And when we stand before the judgement throne, and we WILL ALL stand before that throne, that reason for our failure to do what we should, will not even come up—because it has already been judged and burned up, long before we are. We are not judged by what others do or fail to do—we are judged by what we do or fail to do. We all fall and get up and keep going, and perhaps we fall again, but we get up again and again and again and keep going. Jesus learned obedience by what He suffered, yet we don't think we need to.

Hebrews 5:7-9 HCSB (commentary added)

> [7]During His earthly life, He offered prayers and appeals with loud cries and tears to the One who was able to save Him from death, and He was heard because of His reverence. [8]Though He was God's Son, He learned obedience through what He suffered. [9]After He was perfected, He became the source of eternal salvation for all who obey Him *[to complete, make perfect; to reach the intended goal]*.

We are like a house with many rooms, and we learn something in each of those rooms. Jesus learned by His Prayers and appeals, loud cries and tears, and suffering—and He was heard by God, because He gave God Him due reverence, and respect, and His obedience to His Father, God, kept Him from making those little rooms. An unfinished argument, an emotion held back, a word we feel we need to speak, each of them is another room in the house, which we are—anger out of control that is turned to peace, hate turned to love, rage turned to calm—we are the house or tent or body that houses all of those rooms.

Some rooms are exposed to more light than others and we excel in them, because we are able to see better what we are doing. The closer we get to the light in each of those rooms, the more we see. I want to speak about the rooms in our house—the one we live in, the one we are. I am going to begin with a vision that the Lord gave me.

I was lying upon my bed and saw a vision of a great variety of dogs running down a paved road. Dogs of all breeds and sizes and colors. As the dogs ran, they became young people in their 20's and 30's. They were the ones who were running like dogs in a mad chase on this hardtop road. As they ran, the road changed, and became treacherous and wet, the sky became black and ominous, and soon the road appeared like a narrow ocean with sharp tiny icebergs sticking up everywhere.

The young people paid no attention to the change in the road or the icebergs; they kept running down this narrow ocean road and would not slow down... At the end of the road I saw ominous billowing clouds of black and grey and I saw destruction. They kept running, unabated, by the wet road or the sharp ice protrusions in the roadway, as if they were not concerned that they were there, or that these conditions would have any influence on them.

The reason they started out as dogs is because they were following the pack. They were doing what almost everybody else in the world does. They were comfortable being a part of the pack, fitting into the world system.

Let's talk about the little rooms that we have created in our lives. Have you ever had to go somewhere and right before you arrived at your destination, you and your spouse had a fight? Because she said something that you were unhappy about or you said something she was unhappy about? Because of time constraints and the fast pace of life today, perhaps you tucked it away in one of the little rooms in your mind for discussion or confrontation at a later time. What you have done is grabbed hold of a tiny iceberg, designed to scuttle the ship of your life. What you should have done is let it go when it happened.

Then you got where you were going, and perhaps you heard a poignant message about how things really should be, and at the end of the meeting, because you were not able to do anything about what you heard, you put the information into one of those little rooms, and just tucked it away for later.

Then when you arrived home, perhaps another issue faced you concerning your spouse, kids or job, so the previous issues remain tucked away in those little rooms and you are forced to deal with the pressing issue at hand, thinking, I'll take care of that other one tomorrow, it's getting too late to do it now. Tomorrow comes, and wouldn't you know it, the day begins, and you are faced with yet another issue, and because you are already late for work you put this new issue into one of those little compartments; in one of those little rooms in your heart or your head to deal with later, and off to work you go. I think by now you are getting the idea of where I am going.

The issues you have placed in those little rooms in your head, or your heart were NORMAL size issues that people face, BUT now they had time to grow and expand those little rooms, and what was once little has become somewhat more encompassing. By now the rooms have added some older issues, issues that long ago you recorded in the journal in your mind that were tucked away nicely themselves in other little rooms. When you should have let them go. What is the point? We have brewed a storm in a teacup. The items in those little rooms are now propelling us.

We are now at a place where the ISSUES in those rooms are motivating our thinking and our behavior. We have let the issues become problems, and we've allowed the problems to take dominion or rule over us. When we should have let them go *(see Matthew6:34, Don't worry about tomorrow, today has enough problems of its own)* and depending on what time of the day these issues all decide to open their little doors, we will have a blowup or a blowout. Would you venture a guess as to who would be behind this? The enemy of your souls relies on you and me for his power and authority in the earth. When we abide or dwell on problems they become sin; and when we are dwelling on these sins we have forgotten everything we have worked so hard to learn about faith and we have negated our faith.

satan remembers what he was able to do, before Jesus stripped him of all power and authority, and he also remembers what you have behind door #1 and door #2 and door #3 And you get the idea. He remembers what you said, how you said it and in just what room you left it. He reminds you, "Certainly we don't want to forget this or let this go by." So, we keep a mental journal, and because he needs your authority, he provokes you with you need to do something about these little rooms, and you need to do it RIGHT NOW!! You deserve better than this.

The word teaches us NOT to keep a journal or list of things done against us. The devil gets you to open the doors to the little rooms and remember the journal and now he has been given by

YOU, the power to speak and operate in your life; a power he does not have without you. He has taken an issue and made it a place of dwelling, because your mind has a journal or list of hot buttons that will open each of those little rooms. Ephesians 4:27 tells us not to give the devil a place, but without realizing it, we have done just that. We have given him ground that he can stand upon in our lives; legally. satan will even provide you with the words to say for this confrontation and he only uses the best ones, the juiciest words with the ability and intent to provoke the most response. And all we need to use them is the right HOT BUTTON. A word, look, place.

1 Peter 5:8 KJV Peter has some advice for us:

> [8]Be sober, be vigilant, because your adversary
> the devil, as a roaring lion, walketh about,
> seeking whom he may devour.

I have also included this verse in the NIV, because it has clearly grasped the intent of Peter's letter.

1 Peter 5:8 NIV

> [8]Be self-controlled and alert. Your enemy the
> devil prowls around like a roaring lion looking
> for someone to devour.

The words walketh about [*peripateo*] refer to someone who is making progress, due to the opportunities that have been made available to him during his walk. How are these opportunities made available to him? By our words, our sighs, our attitudes and our demeanor. With each of them, we have given him a place in our lives; we have given him ground upon which to stand.

Now read this with me as it should be read; your enemy who does not know who his prey will be, is making progress in that regard, due to the opportunities that we give him because we fail to control our soul and we are not watchful, we do not guard what we say and do, so, he swallows our potential and sets out to destroy our destiny. When our spirit man is not in control, our soul man rises up and speaks what should never have been allowed to remain in our heart, and out of our mouth it comes — the words he gave us, so that he can use them against us. Typically, we believe that we are the only ones who are going through these problems and no one else is suffering as we are. The last person, who believed that was Elijah, who was told by God that there were 7000 just like him, only better, they weren't complaining. satan is looking for someone — any target who will accept his attack, because he does NOT KNOW. He is waiting for someone to tell him or show him, and that is what Peter said in

1 Peter 5:8 NIV

> [8]Be self-controlled and alert. Your enemy the devil prowls around like a roaring lion looking for someone to devour.

The word roaring means he has raised his voice to create fear. The doctor said, the boss said, the banker said, the spouse said, etc. Fear gives him an opening, and allows him a place to set up camp, and go to war against whoever does not know God or who does know God but has taken their eyes off of God and placed them upon their circumstances; people who do this, say or do things that reveal that they are vulnerable.

Faith leaves when fear comes, because fear is faith in what satan said about your problem. Faith is, believing that God will have His way, and trusting Him to accomplish it. Fear is, believing that the devil will have his way, and trusting him to accomplish it, and many, if not most of us, have been there at some time in our thinking. That means that fear is faith in the devil and expecting his efforts to be successful, and sadly, when things go badly as they often do, we have a faith failure and give place or ground to the enemy of our soul in our thought life and through our words we confirm them.

Our enemy is looking for any opening we will give him, and if we do not give him one, he cannot indiscriminately devour us. He is using the situation that we are involved in, as an opening for him to set up shop. He is looking for a word, a sigh or a grimace or any gesture that shows weakness. The bible uses the term lion for him, because lions have great strength and they are to be regarded as having potential to be dangerous, because of this strength... His roaring is all mouth, until we combine his roaring, which created fear in us, with our words, and when that happens our words create death.

The word in the two translations say he is like or as the lion, but he is neither one. He does have the ability to give us a hard time, and often he does wax eloquent, because he knows the correct words that set us off.

Psalm 34:19 KJV

> ¹⁹Many are the afflictions of the righteous: but
> the LORD delivereth him out of them all.

The word *afflictions* is the strongest reference to hurtful mischief, misery sorrow, calamity and trouble.

Psalms 34:19 tells us, it really does not matter what comes against those in right standing with God—God will snatch them away from it, deliver them from it, preserve them in it, recover them, and save them out of it. Listen to what we just read another time: God will snatch you out of all of what comes against you. All of what comes against you, if you are considered by Him to be in right standing; righteous and if by your words you do not agree with the devil. That means you are repentant and working diligently to keep away from iniquity and sin and are not holding an offense against someone.

For many years we have been learning to watch our words—too many don't. What happens when we don't? God tells us in Deuteronomy, "I will record this day against you." Deuteronomy 30:19, *"I call heaven and earth to record this day against you, that I have set before you, life and death, blessing and cursing: therefore, choose life, that both thou and thy seed may live"* (KJV).

What is God recording? Your every word!! The word record means to bear witness again and again. Listen to this with your heart. The word record means to bear witness again, and again, and again. "You may choose life, or you may choose death, I am giving you the choice." God has said, "It is your words that heaven will record this day and each day—what you have just said into the air, or to your spouse or your child or parent or someone else in anger, or in love or in peace." I am giving you the choice. I will play it again and again. It is all about the little rooms, and what you will say when you open the doors to those little rooms. It is your words that heaven and earth will record, THE ONES you just said to your spouse or parent or child or someone else, even the air, in anger, and what you just muttered as you walked away, OH YES you got the last word alright, and now it is recorded against you.

However, in the spirit world that last BAD word was recorded against you as a curse over your marriage or job or friendship or family relationship, and just how many of those do you think you can chalk up before your marriage or relationships or job have been cursed almost beyond repair? What did you mutter anyway? Will it fix anything or change anything? Was it worth what could soon happen? How does God see that behavior from you? Or how about your sighs; what do they say. God is the one who said He would record it and play it again and again.

That brings up a question: "How long do our words last?"

Matthew 24:35 (KJV) Jesus said:

> [35]"Heaven and earth shall pass away, but my words shall not pass away."

Since I am made in the image of God and He has given me authority in His kingdom on earth to create with my words, 1 John 4:17 as He is so am I, just maybe my words will not pass away either.

How important are words?

John 6:63 (KJV) Jesus said:

> ⁶³It is the spirit that quickeneth; the flesh profiteth nothing: the words that I speak unto you, they are spirit, and they are life.

How important are words?

In John 8:51 Jesus said, when a believer's spirit leaves the body, it goes to Him: "⁵¹Verily, verily, I say unto you, If a man keep [tay-reh'-o 5083] my saying, he shall never see [theh-o-reh'-o 2334] death." The word for keep means hold fast, watch, preserve, guard and obey. [And the word for SEE means to be acquainted with]

Jesus is saying that His words that a man holds fast, and preserves will keep that man from experiencing the sting of death. What about my words? It seems that we as believers cannot get away from that word obey. Jesus is saying that the man who preserves, guards and obeys God's words will never personally become acquainted with his own death. God has given great weight to His words and our words.

Proverbs 18:21 KJV

> ²¹Death and life are in the power of the tongue:
> and they that love it shall eat the fruit thereof.

The church must no longer read that in a matter-of-fact way. Death and life are in the power of the tongue. Look with me at what it tells us about death. The word death used here refers to the cause of death. The physical corruption of the human body and the cause of death and pain are found in the words we use daily. So, the word death in this verse means that we can corrupt our bodies by the words we speak. If the words we speak, as the temple of Holy Spirit will not pass away, then let us choose them with caution.

I think it is way past time to empty those little rooms and repent for keeping something in them. Will you join me in a simple public confession?

> *Father, I confess that I have not been careful with*
> *my words or with my imagination, which has*
> *produced those words.*

I confess I have said things and revealed by my words and actions a lack of faith in what your word declares is mine—forgive me and reverse the curse of those actions and words.

Help me remember this message and let it come to my eyes and ears when I begin to keep or hold in my heart again, those little rooms.

Many believers have been told after we are born again that we have arrived and often that stops our progress toward holiness, but In the world of the spirit, we have just begun, we have just been given access to a totally new world. The phrase "your names are written in Heaven" means you are positioned to accomplish your destiny, so that NOW you can fulfill your calling in the earth and then in heaven when the time comes. You have a place in reserved for you in heaven while you are qualifying for your role in heaven—qualifying while you are on the earth, so function like you have a place in heaven. Earth is a place of qualification for our roles in heaven. Time is merely a blip on the radar screen of ions and ions of eternity. Time is a qualifying period or not, for our roles in heaven. We are either being qualified or disqualified during this period called time.

Every decision we make after we make Jesus our Savior on our way to making Him our Lord is a decision of qualification or disqualification, there is no middle ground. Someday the angel of the Lord will descend from Heaven and declare TIME WILL BE NO MORE, and from that point on ETERNITY begins. From that point on nothing else can be done to change what we have done or have not done.

I cannot imagine the God of the universe allowing us to spend 70 or more years of this vast amount of time called eternity and not have it account for more than just getting into heaven. God is a God of industry, therefore everything we are doing and what we are going through is for qualification for a greater role in eternity. This idea that we go to heaven and float on clouds or sit back and relax is not in keeping with how God thinks. We will be busy in heaven, and not only will we gather in praise and worship, but we will be functioning AND WORKING as the body was intended to function from the beginning. Ask yourself this question. How is MY qualification going? Am I doing my part? NOW is the time to evaluate yourself and make course corrections.

You are part of the body of Christ with equal shares of His life, so it is time to act like it. No longer waiting for the curtain call of the actor that is finished; it is time to move into or onto the stage of our spiritual life.

This Christian life is filled with a great deal more than any of us have realized. If this is not the greatest life in the world, then we are not doing our part to make it so. King David told his son, Solomon, whom history records as the wisest man in the world to heed his advice and that caution and advice extends to us.

1 Chronicles 28:9 (HCSB)

> [9]"As for you, Solomon my son, know the God of your father, and serve Him with a whole heart and a willing mind, for the LORD searches every heart and understands the intention of every thought. If you seek Him, He will be found by you, but if you forsake Him, He will reject you forever."

God said, "If you seek me with all your heart I will be found of you." So, how does God see you or me? He sees us as friends and then warriors and champions and winners, and ultimately as sons. And because He sees us as sons, He has already reserved a place for us in heaven. However, it is up to us to fill the requirements of His expectations for us and move from a sinner saved by Grace to a son who seeks His Father God and whose life is devoted to becoming as Jesus and walking in this life toward perfection

CHAPTER SEVEN

If God sees me the way you say He sees me, then why am I so bruised and beat up. Allow me to share the stories of 5 people who could have said the same thing and yet they functioned from a place or position that revealed that they most likely never said or even though the way many of us do. Does anyone think that Abraham knew how important he would become? Or Moses or Joseph, or Job or Daniel or Esther? That also applies to you and to me—we do not know what our end will be, but we do know that if we follow hard after God and do what His word has told us to do, we will have an end that will have changed not just our life, but many lives around us.

We may never know who paved the way for us, or for whom we paved the way. In God's economy we are here because we are important to His plan. Ezra and Nehemiah could never have achieved what they did had it not been for Esther, Mordecai, and Daniel paving the way for them, and none of these three ever stopped to think that without them, things would have been very different.

You are vital and important, and you may never know to whom or how vital and important you are, but that aside, you were born to fulfill a destiny that no one else was born to fulfill. You cannot quit, because than you will never be who or what God destined you to be and to do. No one writes stories about quitters or writes about those who fail to show up, when they could have made a difference, when all we have to do is show up. Sometimes the people who show up have little more than heart, but I will take heart over all other things, including talent and gifts that do not include heart.

Life and people can change your body—they can change your name—your environment—and even your plans for the future, but they cannot change your heart, and they are not in control of your destiny—God is, if you are partnered with Him.

I am going to share the lives of several whose bodies were changed, and whose names were changed and whose environment was changed and whose hopes and dreams were dashed as if none of it mattered. It did matter to God, and in each case, He had a bigger and better and more perfect plan, a plan that none of them would have ever been able to dream.

Let's begin looking at the lives of people we are all familiar with and who became patriarchs of our faith in God. Abraham was told by God that he would be the father of many nations, and for 23 years, without the manifestation of it, he believed that promise. There were some bumps along the way, but he never doubted God's word or His promise to him.

Ishmael was one of those bumps along the way, that Sara his wife had helped produce, by telling him to bed Hagar after the promise that God gave Abraham was 10 years past any manifestation.

Genesis 17:1-6,15-21 (NIV) God reconfirms the covenant He had made 23 years before, when Abraham was 76:

> [1]When Abram was ninety-nine years old, the LORD appeared to him and said, "I am God Almighty; walk before me and be blameless. [2]I will confirm my covenant between me and you and will greatly increase your numbers."

> [3]Abram fell facedown, and God said to him, [4]"As for me, this is my covenant with you: You will be the father of many nations. [5]No longer will you be called Abram; your name will be Abraham, for I have made you a father of many nations. [6]I will make you very fruitful; I will make nations of you, and kings will come from you.

> [15]God also said to Abraham, "As for Sarai your wife, you are no longer to call her Sarai; her name will be Sarah. [16]I will bless her and will surely give you a son by her. I will bless her so that she will be the mother of nations; kings of peoples will come from her."
>
> [17]Abraham fell facedown; he laughed and said to himself, "Will a son be born to a man a hundred years old? Will Sarah bear a child at the age of ninety?" [18]And Abraham said to God, "If only Ishmael might live under your blessing!"
>
> [19]Then God said, "Yes, but your wife Sarah will bear you a son, and you will call him Isaac. I will establish my covenant with him as an everlasting covenant for his descendants after him.

This sentence reads as God's confirmation of what He has just said, and Abraham took God at His word from this point on.

> [20]And as for Ishmael, I have heard you: I will surely bless him; I will make him fruitful and will greatly increase his numbers. He will be the

father of twelve rulers, and I will make him into a great nation. ²¹But my covenant I will establish with Isaac, whom Sarah will bear to you by this time next year."

For nine months he and Sara were calling themselves father and mother of nations and all their friends and family called them by those names—even without any proof of it being true.

Please do not forget that he and every male in his household had been circumcised immediately after God left his side, as a sign that he believed God, and trusted Him to complete His word.

Genesis 18:10-15 NIV

> ¹⁰Then the LORD said, "I will surely return to you about this time next year, and Sarah your wife will have a son."

> Now Sarah was listening at the entrance to the tent, which was behind him. ¹¹Abraham and Sarah were already old and well advanced in years, and Sarah was past the age of childbearing. ¹²So Sarah laughed to herself as

she thought, "After I am worn out and my master is old, will I now have this pleasure?"

[13]Then the LORD said to Abraham, "Why did Sarah laugh and say, 'Will I really have a child, now that I am old?' [14]Is anything too hard for the LORD? I will return to you at the appointed time next year and Sarah will have a son."

[15]Sarah was afraid, so she lied and said, "I did not laugh."
But he said, "Yes, you did laugh."

Sarah did not believe God, because she looked at the circumstances and knew without a doubt that she was not capable of producing life, and Abraham likewise could not perform.

Abraham did not look at the circumstances any longer, because he believed that God would do exactly as He said, and he was believing it BY HIMSELF, because no one else, even his wife, believed the circumstances could change. Within the year they had Isaac and for the next 50 years Abraham was able to have children, and did have 6 sons by his second wife Keturah.

Everything that God had promised came true and Abraham saw not only that, but he saw the day of Jesus, and Jesus said so in John 8:58, when He said, your father Abraham saw my day and was glad. Those of you who think that you are standing alone are not alone because God is standing with you, but only if you choose to covenant with Him.

Moses had no bible to read and of course neither did Abraham. So, neither one knew about this great cloud of witnesses that we have. We need to see the witnesses as not only watching us, but us watching them, what they did, because they are the witnesses of whom God is. Moses lived for 40 years and never knew God, he only knew about God, and now he has completed another 40 years in the desert wilderness, not knowing God while he is watching sheep. Never knowing that this job of watching sheep will serve him well because he will watch human sheep, and they are even more difficult to watch over. God arrests him at the burning bush and turns his life around and changes everything in his life.

Do you think God knew where he was for the last 80 years?

Abraham and Moses never heard a preacher or a teacher or read a bible, but both men saw God in the creation around them, and heard His voice when He spoke to them, just like it says in

Romans. The Israelites wanted to quit too many times to count, but Moses would not let them. God made mention that He would kill them all and start over with Moses, but Moses said that would not serve the history of God very well.

Moses' brother and sister and every Jew, but Joshua was against Moses at one time or another, in the wilderness and the desert, but that did not move Moses away from what God said was his role in the life.

What about Job?

He was blessed above every other man upon the earth during his lifetime and the richest man in the east, and suddenly all of it is taken away; literally overnight. His sons and daughters are killed in the same day and if that is not enough, all of his servants and all of his thousands of animals, and he owns groups of thousands of animals that are taken or slaughtered as well.

Not enough?

His dearest friends do not even recognize him when they finally arrive, and are so moved by what they see, that they cannot speak for 7 days. His body is full of boils that are from his feet to the top of his head and Job has fever, and he is so thin one wonders; what is keeping him alive. When they arrive, they find him in ashes, cutting open his boils to get them to drain.

His wife and he had to bury all of their children with their own hands after they were killed, and now he sits alone, because his wife, his partner and best friend, has told him to curse God and die. His comments to her are simple and direct "even if God takes my life, I will trust Him". So, if you are ever feeling down and out and really low, and you are whining about it, and say that you feel like Job, go wash your mouth out with soap.

There are some who have said that all of this took place within a year; I do not know how long it took. What I do know is that he is a witness to the fact that God is faithful, and God knows who you are, and where you are. It does not matter what you or I think about what is going on in our lives, God is very present, and if we will remain in covenant with Him and stay true, we will become victorious and fulfill our destiny.

Job had no example, no bible and no one who believed in him, not even his closest friends.

Job 42:5, 10-17 NIV

> [5]My ears had heard of you,
> but now my eyes have seen you.

¹⁰After Job had prayed for his friends, the LORD made him prosperous again and gave him twice as much as he had before. ¹¹All his brothers and sisters and everyone who had known him before came and ate with him in his house. They comforted and consoled him over all the trouble the LORD had brought upon him, and each one gave him a piece of silver and a gold ring. ¹²The LORD blessed the latter part of Job's life more than the first. He had fourteen thousand sheep, six thousand camels, a thousand yoke of oxen and a thousand donkeys. ¹³And he also had seven sons and three daughters. ¹⁴The first daughter he named Jemimah, the second Keziah and the third Keren-Happuch. ¹⁵Nowhere in all the land were there found women as beautiful as Job's daughters, and their father granted them an inheritance along with their brothers.

¹⁶After this, Job lived a hundred and forty years; he saw his children and their children to the fourth generation. ¹⁷And so he died, old and full of years.

And what about Joseph? Taken from his family at age 17, put in pit and then sold to slavers, Joseph is now gone from his family and believes that he will never see them again.

Genesis 37:36 NIV

> [36]Meanwhile, the Midianites sold Joseph in Egypt to Potiphar, one of Pharaoh's officials, the captain of the guard.

The slavers sold him to the captain of the guard, a man named Potiphar who worked directly for Pharaoh. He is so trustworthy that Potiphar eventually places him over all that he has.

Genesis 39:6-7,12,16-20 NIV

> [6]So he left in Joseph's care everything he had; with Joseph in charge, he did not concern himself with anything except the food he ate.
>
> Now Joseph was well built and handsome, [7]and after a while his master's wife took notice of Joseph and said, "Come to bed with me!"

¹²She caught him by his cloak and said, "Come to bed with me!" But he left his cloak in her hand and ran out of the house.

¹⁶She kept his cloak beside her until his master came home. ¹⁷Then she told him this story: "That Hebrew slave you brought us came to me to make sport of me. ¹⁸But as soon as I screamed for help, he left his cloak beside me and ran out of the house."

¹⁹When his master heard the story his wife told him, saying, "This is how your slave treated me," he burned with anger. ²⁰Joseph's master took him and put him in prison, the place where the king's prisoners were confined.

It is Important to know that Potiphar was a normal male when he married Zuleika, and was forced to be castrated when he was promoted to the control of the King's household police force as ALL who came close to the harem were forced to be. Joseph was never asked what actually happened any more than we would ask a wheelbarrow or a donkey what happened to them, because Joseph was a slave and slaves have no opinion.

Joseph could have been put in the debtor's prison or the common prison, but instead he was put in the prison near Potiphar's house, so that he was safe from harm and death. Potiphar could have had him killed or beaten or castrated, but he did none of it. It is my opinion that Potiphar knew in his heart that Joseph was innocent, and his wife was the aggressor, but Joseph did not know how or what Potiphar knew or felt. Joseph had no bible to read and no one to be accountable to, but it did not matter to Joseph, he was accountable to his father's God; the God he had made his own. He heard stories about how his father wrestled with an angel and how his grandfather had honored God for many years, and he believed so strongly that when he was taken at age 17 and found himself in prison, NEVER having broken any law, he remained true to God.

None of his brothers believed and no one that he had met since he was taken believed in God, but that did not matter to him, he did with all his heart. Joseph remained true to God without ever having had a visitation from God or angels or a word from a prophet and regardless of the trials and temptations that were thrown in his face, he held true to what he learned from his patriarchs.

No bible, no examples, NO ONE who believes what he believes, and one of the most beautiful women in the world is trying to seduce him; her name is Zuleika, and she was well known in the East for her beauty. Every day, day after day, she would present herself in front of him, totally naked, as she worshipped her sun god, Ra. One day she grabbed him and attempted to force him to lay with her. He refused and ran away, and because he did the RIGHT thing, he was put into prison, where he remained for several years, during which time he became the jailors most trusted helper. You all know the story of how he interpreted Pharaoh's dream and became the #2 man in the empire.

Eventually his brothers need grain, because of famine, and they come to Egypt not knowing that Joseph is the man who controls all the grain.

Genesis 42:7-9 NIV

> [7]As soon as Joseph saw his brothers, he recognized them, but he pretended to be a stranger and spoke harshly to them. "Where do you come from?" he asked.
>
> "From the land of Canaan," they replied, "to buy food."

> [8]Although Joseph recognized his brothers they did not recognize him. [9]Then he remembered his dreams about them...

He remembered his dreams. Please <u>notice</u> he remembered his dreams NOT the evil they did to him.

Gensis 45:1,5 NIV

> [1]Then Joseph could no longer control himself before all his attendants, and he cried out, "Have everyone leave my presence!" So, there was no one with Joseph when he made himself known to his brothers.

Joseph could not allow anyone to know what they had done, or Egypt would have retaliated against them—Joseph was the Savior of the nation and the then known world.

> [5]And now, do not be distressed and do not be angry with yourselves for selling me here, because it was to save lives that God sent me ahead of you.

No anger and no retribution and if anyone had a reason for both, Joseph did. They kidnapped him and took him away from his family, changed his name and his environment, and made him to appear just like them. Taken and made a slave, imprisoned and falsely accused, and he never retaliated, even though he could have. He never quit being what he knew in his heart he could be—no matter what anyone did to him.

What about Daniel, who lived 70 years in Babylonian captivity under 4 different kings—all of whom were tyrants?

Daniel 1:1,3,6-7 NIV

> ¹In the third year of the reign of Jehoiakim king of Judah, Nebuchadnezzar king of Babylon came to Jerusalem and besieged it.
>
> ³Then the king ordered Ashpenaz, chief of his court officials, to bring in some of the Israelites from the royal family and the nobility—
>
> ⁶Among these were some from Judah: Daniel, Hananiah, Mishael and Azariah. ⁷The chief official gave them new names: to Daniel, the name Belteshazzar; to Hananiah, Shadrach; to Mishael, Meshach; and to Azariah, Abednego.

Daniel's name means God is judge. Hananiah means God is gracious. Azariah means God is my help. And Mishael means who is like God. The new names they were given contradict the names they were originally given by their parents. Daniel becomes Belteshazzar, Bel an Egyptian god will protect. Hananiah becomes Shadrach, inspired of Aku, an Egyptian god. Mishael becomes Meshach, belonging to Aku and Azariah becomes Abed-nego, a servant of Nego, another Egyptian god.

Others were able to change the names of these men, but they could not change their hearts. They also changed their environment but still they could not change them. Just as soon as they arrived in this new land, they were all castrated, but that did not change their hearts.

So much for the plans of Daniel and his friends, who were taken with him. Daniel was taken from his family and land of his birth. He had grown up in the house of royalty and was a prince with a bright future and plans of having his own children to pass along his wisdom and skills and holdings, but that was abruptly taken away.

In the 3rd year of Jehoiakim, king of Israel, God judged his nation, because of this evil king, and took the nation away from this foolish king, and Daniel and others were taken to Babylon,

NEVER AGAIN to see their parents or their families or the land of their nativity. America is beginning to see how it is really important who is in charge of a nation. Daniel will remain a captive here for the rest of his life, which is about 70 more years. Instead of crying and saying, 'woe is me', they took away my manhood and my ability to have children; he made the best of his situation. He did not whine as many children would whine, because their parents took away their cell phone, baseball, basketball, computer, football or TV.

Daniel was a young teenager, perhaps 15 or 16 and instead of behaving badly, he becomes the example for all others. His destiny, the one that God had prepared for him would NEVER have been realized if he behaved like so many that we see. God would have been forced to pass over him and select another person, one who has the character and moral fiber that He is looking for. God is always looking for someone in whom He can show Himself strong.

The new king and tyrant that Daniel is now required to serve, has a dream and Daniel and his three friends have gotten use to their new roles in this very different land.

By the way, Arab castration of male slaves has a 92% mortality rate, So, it becomes obvious that God is watching these 4 young men who have made Him Lord of their lives.

King Nebuchadnezzar has a dream, and all the wise men have been called and are under the penalty of death, if no one can give the king the answer to his dream, but Daniel has not been called nor have his three friends. God gives Daniel the interpretation of the dream after he and his three friends get together to pray and ask God for the interpretation.

Daniel 2:26-28 NIV

> [26]The king asked Daniel (also called Belteshazzar), "Are you able to tell me what I saw in my dream and interpret it?"
>
> [27]Daniel replied, "No wise man, enchanter, magician or diviner can explain to the king the mystery he has asked about, [28]but there is a God in heaven who reveals mysteries. He has shown King Nebuchadnezzar what will happen in days to come. Your dream and the visions that passed through your mind as you lay on your bed are these…

And Daniel reveals the dream's interpretation. Daniel is openly respectful of the man who gave orders to kill all the wise men including him and all the others without cause.

Daniel 2:46-49 NIV

> [46]Then King Nebuchadnezzar fell prostrate before Daniel and paid him honor and ordered that an offering and incense be presented to him. [47]The king said to Daniel, "Surely your God is the God of gods and the Lord of kings and a revealer of mysteries, for you were able to reveal this mystery."
>
> [48]Then the king placed Daniel in a high position and lavished many gifts on him. He made him ruler over the entire province of Babylon and placed him in charge of all its wise men. [49]Moreover, at Daniel's request the king appointed Shadrach, Meshach and Abednego administrators over the province of Babylon, while Daniel himself remained at the royal court.

Time passes and as it always is with tyrants, and men who think they are above God's laws, the king does something else that requires all of the subjects to be politically correct or face death in the furnace. Daniel's three friends will not bow to Nebuchadnezzar's new statue of himself, so, they are given a second chance, to which they reply, with great restraint and respect, 'our God is able to save us your majesty, but if He chooses not to, we will continue to serve Him and never bow down to your statue'.

Everyone in the land has now heard how a fourth man was seen walking in the furnace with Daniel's three friends, and they have been released unharmed and the king has publically acknowledged that their God is God. This king has another dream and once again Daniel interprets it. Again, time passes, and Nebuchadnezzar forgets that he is not God, and his time comes to an end. His son Nabonidus, and his grandson Belshazzar rule the land of Babylon as co-regents. The grandson is the one we have all heard about. He is the king when the hand of God writes on the wall, "MENE MENE TEKEL UPHARSON." Darius the Mede takes the kingdom from the grandson and puts 120 princes over all of the provinces and Daniel is made president over all of them.

Daniel 6:4-5 NIV

> [4]At this, the administrators and the satraps tried to find grounds for charges against Daniel in his conduct of government affairs, but they were unable to do so. They could find no corruption in him, because he was trustworthy and neither corrupt nor negligent. [5]Finally these men said, "We will never find any basis for charges against this man Daniel unless it has something to do with the law of his God."

Apparently, Daniel did not allow the government's national rule about no prayer in schools at games or at public functions bother him. Apparently, he would rather continue in his actions before God, as opposed to becoming mediocre, just like everyone else who chose to be politically correct. Daniel chose courage and faithfulness, so that God could find in him a man who could be trusted to stand, when all others were afraid of the government's folly and law decreeing no prayer in public.

Daniel 6:4-5,13 NIV

> [13]Then they said to the king, "Daniel, who is one of the exiles from Judah, pays no attention to

you, O king, or to the decree you put in writing. He still prays three times a day."

The politically correct organization came to the king and ratted out Daniel. I found it interesting that Daniel has been in politically important posts; never failing to serve well even once, for over 40 years and the Medes and Persians still called him the foreigner. The politicians never accepted him—WOW can you imagine any politician today NOT following in goose step behind the crowd—.

Daniel 6:16,19-21 NIV

> [16]So the king gave the order, and they brought Daniel and threw him into the lions' den. The king said to Daniel, "May your God, whom you serve continually, rescue you!"

> [19]At the first light of dawn, the king got up and hurried to the lions' den. [20]When he came near the den, he called to Daniel in an anguished voice, "Daniel, servant of the living God, has your God, whom you serve continually, been able to rescue you from the lions?" [21]Daniel answered, "O king, live forever!

Daniel would not allow those who castrated him and made him a captive for the rest of his life, change him. He would not give into the hatred of others around him, because they still considered him a foreigner, after over 40 years of perfect service to those who ruled over him or lived under him. He responded to the king who put him in the lion's den with grace and respect and gave him honor. Do you suppose God knew where he was all of this time? How do you think the lion's den would have turned out, if when Daniel was thrown in he was still angry and carrying the offense—I don't think the result would have been the same.

Finally, we will look at Esther. There is a time to speak and a time to be silent and Esther knew when to do both.

Esther 2:7-9 NIV

> [7]Mordecai had a cousin named Hadassah, whom he had brought up because she had neither father nor mother. This girl, who was also known as Esther, was lovely in form and features, and Mordecai had taken her as his own daughter when her father and mother died.

> [8]When the king's order and edict had been proclaimed, many girls were brought to the citadel of Susa and put under the care of Hegai. Esther also was taken to the king's palace and entrusted to Hegai, who had charge of the harem. [9]The girl pleased him and won his favor. Immediately he provided her with her beauty treatments and special food. He assigned to her seven maids selected from the king's palace and moved her and her maids into the best place in the harem.

We see immediately why Hegai gave his favor to Esther—it was her character, openly seen by her behavior, that earned her favor.

Esther 2:10,19-20 NIV

> [10]Esther had not revealed her nationality and family background, because Mordecai had forbidden her to do so.
>
> [19]When the virgins were assembled a second time, Mordecai was sitting at the king's gate. [20]But Esther had kept secret her family

background and nationality just as Mordecai had told her to do, for she continued to follow Mordecai's instructions as she had done when he was bringing her up.

It would be helpful to know that over 127 hundred virgins were brought to the castle to vie for the position vacated by Vashti the queen. By reading the story we find that the idea of WHAT'S IN IT FOR ME, did not originate in America. It has become the loudest cry we hear in America, and we hear it daily. "What's in it for me?" We see it in almost all politicians, we use to see it in the white house, but not now; for the first time since Ronald Reagan. We see it in school, sports, churches, and even in the family. The young virgins in this account of Esther behaved in that fashion, but Esther did not.

In each of these places I mentioned there are some who refuse to bend their thoughts to be like the world, not many, but there are a few, and sometimes it only takes one to change the world. Esther was that one. Esther was taken from her home to the palace without her consent; she was between 14 and 16 years old, a teenager. Nobody asked her what she wanted or if this was acceptable to her—no one cared—no one except God and her cousin Mordecai. Even though God cared about her and was watching over her, she did not know it. She had never heard His voice or had an angelic visit, and no prophet had given her a word. She only knew what she heard from her parents, now dead, and her cousin Mordecai. She never read a bible or a Christian novel or heard a self-help tape or CD. She never watched Beth Moore, Jane Hamon or Joyce Meyer on TV.

She never complained or rebelled or pouted when everything that was hers was taken and we know that by how others responded to her. No cell phone and no texting. No TV and no computer. No car, no date night and no hanging out at the mall with friends. Even her name was changed to Persian Star or Ishtar. Taken to a hostile environment where she is competing with over 127 other girls for one night with the king that would determine her life from then on. One night with a famous tyrant with a reputation for war and killing. He made it a law that if you entered the hall without request you would lose your head. She has one shot—one night only with the king and if he is not overwhelmed by her, and with her, in this one night, she will be sent back to the harem, and never again have a man's arms around her and no children to love and nurture. She will stay in the harem with the others until she dies an old maid.

We don't know where she was in the queue, the lineup—we only know that whatever she did and whatever he saw and felt on that special night—the king stopped looking after he was with her.

Now, do you suppose that God had any involvement in that night? God was watching over her as he had always done and now it was her time to shine and she was born for a time such as this, but she did not know it, until her cousin told her that perhaps she was born for this hour in history. She did not know that, in the many months prior during her preparation. The account we have of Esther takes place 30 years before the return of the exiles under Ezra and Nehemiah. Their successes would never have been possible without Esther and Mordecai and Daniel paving the way. Not one of them knew how important they were—not one.

If we don't have a heart to try and keep trying, we will never know what God sees when He sees us and the plan He wrote in the book about us that rests with Him in heaven will not be accomplished and we will NOT HEAR "well done good and faithful servant, enter into the joys of the Lord." Winners never quit and quitters never win. They can change your body, and they can change your name. They can change your environment and stop all your plans for the future, but they cannot change your heart—ONLY YOU CAN DO THAT. You are the only person on earth in control of your destiny, they are not.

When you are partnered with God and have accepted Him as your Lord as well as your Savior and live a life that brings honor to Him, then you have covenanted with Him.

Then, just like these examples of those who never knew we would be reading about them and calling them heroes of the faith, you will be someone we will all read about in time to come.

So, how God sees you and me... is up to us.

Made in United States
Orlando, FL
25 July 2025